"My husband and I were on the 15-year plan…taking almost 15 years before we began to understand one another. I wouldn't recommend that plan for anyone. Instead I would wholeheartedly recommend Jay Payleitner's book *52 Things Husbands Need from Their Wives*. Wives—read it, apply it, and begin today to understand the man in your life."

—**Kendra Smiley,** speaker and author of
Do Your Kids a Favor…Love Your Spouse and other books

"As wives, we can choose to be encouragers for our husbands just as much as we can choose to be discouragers. Jay Payleitner gives us the inside scoop on what every husband needs. His biblically based perspective and end-of-the-chapter takeaways make this book a practical relationship builder for any couple."

—**Karol Ladd,** author of *Positive Life Principles for Women*

"Jay's giving away our secrets, and we thank him for it. This is an insightful read, directed to women but educational for all of us, and a practical, user-friendly tool for any wife wanting to better understand the creature she's joined to."

—**Joe Dallas,** author and speaker

"Very to the point of what a woman needs to know about her man. After reading these 52 insights, you will better understand that your spouse isn't so weird after all."

—**Emilie Barnes,** speaker, author, and
founder of "More Hours In My Day"

"As military families we spend so much valuable time apart from one another. Knowing how to give my husband what he needs—together or apart—is a treasure. On behalf of all wives, thank you, Jay, for your insight and transparency on the one true gift we all can share—love."

—**Tara Crooks,** cofounder of Army Wife Network,
coauthor of *1001 Things to Love about Military Life*

"Husbands, step up to being the spiritual leader in your homes. Start by seeking first the kingdom of God over your own kingdom, and cherishing your wife. Then give your wife a copy of this book by Jay Payleitner. I guarantee you that your marriage will be for the glory of God."

—**Harry W. Schaumburg,** DMin, author of
Undefiled: Redemption from Sexual Sin, Restoration for Broken Relationships

"This little book is a treasure trove of wisdom and advice for any woman who wants to understand her husband better. Simple (just like your husband) in its approach, it gives an excellent snapshot of what's inside the heart and soul of a man. I highly recommend it!"

—**Rick Johnson,** bestselling author of *Becoming Your Spouse's Better Half*
and *How to Talk So Your Husband Will Listen—and Listen So Your Husband Will Talk*

"Wives, you have great power to help your husband feel confident as he faces life's battles. And your encouragement can be a huge asset to him becoming a great husband and father. Jay's *52 Things Husbands Need from Their Wives* will help you understand your man."

—**Carey Casey,** CEO of The National Center for Fathering
and author of *Championship Fathering*

"Jay has done it again. He continues to give us unique insight into building strong family relationships."

—**Dan Seaborn,** president and founder of Winning At Home, Inc.

52 THINGS HUSBANDS NEED FROM THEIR WIVES

JAY PAYLEITNER

HARVEST HOUSE PUBLISHERS
EUGENE, OREGON

Cover by Left Coast Design, Portland, Oregon

Cover photo © Yari Arcurs / Shutterstock

Jay Payleitner is represented by MacGregor Literary Inc. of Hillsboro, Oregon.

52 THINGS HUSBANDS NEED FROM THEIR WIVES
Copyright © 2013 by Jay Payleitner
Published by Harvest House Publishers
Eugene, Oregon 97402
www.harvesthousepublishers.com

Library of Congress Cataloging-in-Publication Data
    Payleitner, Jay K.
    52 things husbands need from their wives / Jay Payleitner.
        pages cm
    ISBN 978-0-7369-5485-3 (pbk.)
    ISBN 978-0-7369-5486-0 (eBook)
    1. Marriage. 2. Marriage—Religious aspects—Christianity. 3. Wives—Conduct of life.
    4. Husbands—Psychology. I. Title. II. Title: Fifty-two things husbands need from their wives.
    HQ734.P3169 2013
    306.872'2—dc23
                                                                    2013012426

14 15 16 17 18 19 20 21 / BP-CD / 10 9 8 7 6 5 4

To my bride, Rita—
for loving me
despite, through, and because of
all my faults.

Acknowledgments

I need to thank all the women over the years who have modeled the art and science of being a wonderful wife.

My mom, Marguerite. My sisters and sister-in-law, Mary Kay, Sue, and Chris. My daughters-in-law, Rachel, Lindsay, and Megan. And my own awesomely awesome bride of more than three decades, Rita.

There are also quite a few other women I know who are divinely supportive wives. I am thinking of dozens of Rita's girlfriends from church and the community, from among those sitting in bleachers and volunteering at school, and from the neighborhoods in which we've lived. Also, I've come to really appreciate the wives of all the guys in my men's Bible study groups over the years. Some of you I may have never even met, but your husbands speak well of you!

Beyond my family, individuals who have contributed directly to this project include Geri Fuehring, Jack Goldthwaite, Mike Hurn, Ken Anderson, Gary Sanders, Randy Burggraf, Bob Anderson, Dave George, Dennis O'Malley, Dick Graff, John Hrivnak, John Waters, Mitch Belon, Tom Pate, Terry Jones, and Ron Basar.

Strategic encouragement and support came from fellow author Karol Ladd, my agent Sandra Bishop, and my colleagues Carey Casey and Brock Griffin at The National Center for Fathering. I also cannot say enough good stuff about Paul Gossard, Terry Glaspey, Bob Hawkins Jr., and the entire team at Harvest House Publishers.

I am more than grateful to the pastors and event planners who have invited me to encourage, laugh with, and challenge diverse groups of dads and husbands. I have no idea whether this book—for wives—will lead to my speaking in auditoriums in which I am the only male. Yikes.

Finally, of course, to our heavenly Father, who created marriage as the perfect building block for families, neighborhoods, communities, nations, and our world.

Contents

Asking You to Trust Me

I love strong, confident women. My wife, Rita, has always been smart, virtuous, and forthright. Her confidence came after realizing how much she had to offer as a mother and as an advocate for strong families. Today she's an alderman sitting as one of ten council members for a city of about 35,000 people. Rita is the best mom in the world as well as a new grandmother(!), and she makes me a better man.

I have three daughters-in-law. Rachel, Lindsay, and Megan proved they were smart when they chose to marry a Payleitner man. And every moment we spend together as a family reveals an expanse of unique gifts and abilities in each of them.

My one daughter is stunning in her ability to stand up for what she believes and state her case. Rae Anne is beautiful, courageous, and tenacious. She's currently at West Point. Need I say more?

I love these women unconditionally. They each have strengths I do not have.

As you dig into this book, you're going to find that I am a cheerleader for marriage, for husbands, and for wives. God's design for perpetuating the human race is nothing short of a miracle. It's a man and woman who commit to each other for life, work side by side, and sacrifice for each other. Such is the building block of healthy families, neighborhoods, communities, and countries.

As much as I believe in marriage, this was actually a difficult book to write. Because it requires me to talk to women. Usually that's something I enjoy doing. But I'm not just chitchatting here. I'm speaking into their lives, supposedly telling them what to do. In my earlier book, *52 Things Wives Need from Their Husbands*, I felt quite comfortable coming alongside men and saying, "Come on, dude. You know what your wife needs. Stop being a selfish jerk. Just do it. Be the man. Be the husband your wife needs." In my natural tone, no guy is going to be offended by that.

But I can't use that tone with women I don't know. I can't say, "Hey babe, just give your old man what he wants." Yikes. That sounds creepy, doesn't it?

So I figure the first step in gaining your trust is to introduce myself. Hi, I'm Jay. I'm a dad of five and husband of one. And a new grandpa. I'm 55, which seems young sometimes and old other times. In high school I wrestled and did some acting. I was a Sigma Pi at Illinois Wesleyan University. After college, I worked some crazy jobs. (Chapter 5 tells that story.) I married my high-school sweetheart, and we live in the same town where we met. My dad passed away two years ago and I miss him. Mom is settled in to a retirement center. We go to the big nondenominational church on the edge of town, where I volunteer at AWANA and other youth stuff. For our kids, we've cheered and applauded hundreds of games, matches, and concerts and also loved on ten foster babies. I think this is my eleventh book, and I still love hearing from readers and speaking at events.

So there. I'm just a regular guy who looks at old truths in fresh ways and applies them to marriage and parenting. Following in my established tradition, I present 52 things your husband may (or may not) need from you. Worth noting, three or four of these are actually flip-flopped chapters stolen from my book written for husbands. Same issue and same point of potential conflict, but seen from the opposite perspective.

With any luck several of these short chapters will help you connect or reconnect with your husband, which makes it worth my effort and worth your investment of a few hours and a few bucks. If not, let me know. And if I say something boneheaded, let me know that too.

Signed,

Your new friend, Jay

What no wife of a writer understands is that a writer
is working when he's staring out the window.

—BURTON RASCOE

A Husband Needs His Wife…

To Slide Over Next to Him

A husband and wife are driving down a country road. They're a few years older than you are now. He's behind the wheel. The pavement and cornfields are passing by. She breaks the silence with a sigh and says, "Remember when we were younger and we used to sit right next to each other in the car?" "I remember," the husband replies after a moment, "but you know, I haven't moved."

It's a story from way before seat-belt laws, but the sentiment still carries a bushel of truth. Men—the good ones like your husband—travel down the road of life with a sense of purpose and focus. We're not out drinking every night. We do our best to bring home a paycheck and be a good father. An affair is not an option. Neither is divorce.

Admittedly, sometimes on the road of life we're preoccupied with getting to the next destination. We watch for speed traps, get miffed at other drivers, and monitor the vehicle's performance. Sometimes we get distracted by a billboard, slow down to see the wreckage of someone else's accident, or take our eyes off the road to watch an eagle swoop over a canyon lake.

But our deepest need on this very real journey is for our bride to slide over close and tell us—just once in a while—that we're doing a good job. That we're appreciated. That you look up to us and need us.

I know that's not easy. Women today are even more distracted than men. You're receiving mixed messages and sending out mixed signals. Your husband wants to give you everything your heart desires, but he's not sure what that is. Some days it's a satisfying career, some days it's a houseful of babies. When you get a $3000 bonus or commission, we don't know whether to suggest a new washer/dryer or a week in Aruba. Would you rather we cleaned the carpets this weekend or took you on a picnic? Do you want us to be more sensitive and watch more chick flicks? Or would we be more attractive to you if we got a Harley and a bad-boy tattoo?

While you're sorting out your fantasies, we're just two feet away and hoping you'll ask us to join you in the journey. We want to partner in your dream. We can be your own personal cheerleader or your sidekick or your shining knight...if only you would slide next to us and tell us what you want.

So how did we get here—two feet and two miles apart?

Think back not too long ago. Remember that boy you married? The handsome young man who caught your eye. The boy you wanted to kiss, but demurely let him make the first move? The boy who taught you to love in brand-new ways. Romantic love. Committed love. Crazy love. Eternal love. Silly love. You may be thinking, *Where did that boy go?*

Ladies, he's right there. That boy is inches away. He's looking down the same road and going the same direction. He's committed to sharing your life and sharing your bed. By the way, he's asking the same question. *Where did that girl go?*

Women of strength and courage, don't be shy. Slide over and let him put his arm around your shoulder. You can even ask him to pull the car over. Look into his eyes, maybe for the first time in a long time. Tell him you're glad you married him. Tell him you need him.

Be the girl. Be the boy. Expect no less than to make each other's hopes and dreams come true.

Takeaway

You did not marry to live separate lives.

> *"Love is as strong as death, its jealousy unyielding as the grave. It burns like blazing fire, like a mighty flame. Many waters cannot quench love; rivers cannot sweep it away."*
>
> —SONG OF SONGS 8:6-7

A Husband Needs His Wife...

To Know His Likes

Here are some things I like: down pillows, sock monkeys, petting doggies, warm feet, a good chopped salad, grilled pork chops, strawberry-rhubarb pie, my entire family all around one table, my entire family all in one pew, bookstores, boxers, brick sidewalks, holding hands with my wife, stopping on the stairs with her one step above for a kiss, comfy jeans, campfires, well-formed quotations, meaningful song lyrics, "The Star-Spangled Banner," watching my kids compete, beef jerky, black Sharpies, bending paper clips, a good pair of scissors, finding a piece of Scripture that applies to a real-life challenge, lying in the grass on a sunny day, strolling a flea market or art fair with my wife, son, and daughter-in-law, etcetera.

It's fun to think about the stuff that makes me smile, satisfies a deep need, or moves my heart. I've never before created such a list. It feels a little decadent, a little selfish. But really this list is a gift to my bride, Rita. She is already well aware of most of my likes (and dislikes). But some may surprise her. When she sees this list—printed here for all the world to see—that will instantly strengthen our relationship. At least it will if she chooses to use the list to her advantage.

Now some of you are thinking the best way for Rita to use any item on this list is as a bribe or a trade-off. "If she makes Jay pork chops and strawberry-rhubarb pie, then she can spend the next afternoon at the day spa." "If she makes sure Jay has a supply of paper clips to bend, maybe he won't notice the dent in the garage door."

You may even be thinking you should make a list for your own husband so you can use it to con him, distract him, or bribe him into giving you some of the things you like. But that's not it at all. No doubt, it's popular to play the game, "If I give him what he likes, he'll give me what I like." But that is no way to run a marriage. The goal is to fully integrate the idea of "two becoming one." A verse that appears in the Bible three times—Genesis chapter 2, Matthew chapter 19, and Ephesians chapter 5—reminds us that "a man will leave his father and mother and be united to his wife, and the two will become one flesh."

United as one flesh? How does that apply here? Maybe think of it this way—*If I give him what he likes, it gives me joy as well.*

Making sense? No? It makes total sense to me, but perhaps that is because I started this chapter out with a list specific to my likes. Many of those items are linked to a connection I have with Rita. Such as when we stand and sing the national anthem. When I catch her eye and we smile across a campfire. When we sit in a pew with our five kids, three daughters-in-law, and grandson between us; we may be literally 20 feet apart, but we're closer than ever. When I'm about to sign something and she brings me just the right black Sharpie. When she lets me have the good down pillow.

I'm pretty sure that if you make a similar list for your husband, it will all be clear. Don't just do it in your head. Get out a yellow pad or open a new Word doc and just start thinking about what makes your husband smile. Or ask him to make the list with you!

Now even though my list is public knowledge, I urge you to keep yours private. There may very well be a few items that really shouldn't be seen by anyone but you and him. As a matter of fact, I left a few of those things off my list. They're between Rita and me.

By the way, don't forget to make a list of your own to share with your husband. I know he'll appreciate it. It may come in real handy on Christmas, Valentine's Day, your birthday. Or maybe later today.

Takeaway

There are things you know about your husband that no one else in the world knows. Which means you are the best person in the world to fill his needs and desires. Which makes marriage different than any other relationship in the world. All part of God's plan.

"When you love someone, all your saved-up wishes start coming out."
—ELIZABETH BOWEN (1899–1973)

A Husband Needs His Wife…

To Expect Some Flaws

I refuse to assemble Ikea furniture. I load the dishwasher wrong. I leave newspapers scattered on the kitchen table. A cup of caffeinated coffee after 6 p.m. will keep me tossing and turning in our shared bed until 2 a.m. According to a recent MRI, my knees need to be replaced. I'm not as patient as I need to be. I like my mom's chili better than my wife's. I like dairy products, but they gurgle my tummy, with unpleasant results. I have sharp toenails.

In other words, I am not the perfect husband. As a matter of fact, I have dozens more flaws that I'm not going to reveal in these pages. To be clear, we're not talking about any of the four A's—abuse, adultery, addiction, or abandonment—which go way beyond the definition of "flaw." Each one of those challenges is a type of brokenness that needs repair. We'll wrestle with some of those issues in later chapters, and more than likely they'll require some professional counseling.

But my flaws—and hopefully the flaws exhibited by your dear husband—don't fall in those categories. Instead, we're more likely to be an occasional thoughtless jerk, pompous blowhard, selfish oaf, lazy bum, or unappreciative dolt. You're occasionally frustrated with us, and rightfully so. But if Rita has been able to put up with me for more than 30 years, I'm thinking you can do the same for the slightly dented package you married.

First, I must say that even though I began this chapter with a partial list of my flaws, don't begin making a similar list for your husband. If it's short, you'll feel bad for judging him. If it's long, you'll stir up feelings that can be very counterproductive.

My recommendation is to wait until one of those minor shortcomings comes to the surface and then deal with it in one of four ways.

Choose to overlook. This is really not as hard as you may think. If once in a while he forgets to use a coaster, wipe his feet, or lower the toilet seat, is it really that big a deal? Is the rare minor infraction worth an evening of tension in the air? If it's a longtime habit and he's slowly improving, don't pounce on the occasional slip-up. And, if he has dairy allergies or a receding hairline, please cut him some slack.

Choose to mention with love. You hate nagging even more than we hate hearing you nag. So—when possible—figure out a way to tell us your desires or point out our flaw in the sweetest way imaginable. Make it a game. Put a positive spin on your instructive instruction. We'll get the message.

"Sweetie Pie, I will make sure we have plenty of your favorite cold beverage on hand if you'll promise to drop the empties in the recycling bin. Deal?"

"Your mom couldn't come over to make chili tonight, so you're going to have to endure my recipe. But I did get the saltines you like. Okay?"

A word of warning about trying to change your hubby with words that sound positive but really aren't. That can quickly turn into passive-aggressive behavior. If you're making demands through clenched teeth, don't kid yourself. You're not smiling, you're attacking. And that never works.

Choose to turn a negative into a positive. This response allows you to be proactive. Take his lemons and make lemonade. If he prefers his mom's chili recipe, don't get mad. Instead, vow to find a recipe even better than your mother-in-law's. If he constantly loses his car keys, give him a key fob with a remote locator as a gift. If he dozes during Sunday-morning sermons, try attending Saturday-evening service or find a church with a more relevant teaching pastor. When his flaw vanishes you can take half the credit. After all, you're not adversaries, you're partners.

Choose to cherish. Have you ever met a widow who talks about her beloved husband's flaws with a slight smile and a twinkle in her eye? She actually misses the boot prints across her kitchen floor and the whiskers in the sink. She would give anything to feel the irritating scratch of his rough beard on her cheek. Don't expect to cherish your husband's flaws until at least a couple decades of marriage. But Rita and I laugh about how so many of the little things that once caused boorish conflict are now endearing quirks that we truly hold dear. If you've been married just a few years, that's probably hard to believe. But stick it out and you'll be amazed at how a lifetime of loving commitment can change your perspective.

Wives, did you notice that each one of those action points begins with the word *choose*? That's right. When conflict arises, quite often you have a choice to make. When you finally realize your husband isn't perfect, your best course of action is to take a few steps back and remember your vows: "For better or worse." Then carefully choose your course of action. For now, your husband's behavior may not be part of the "better." But if his "worse" happens to be a dirty sink, forgetting to call, or socks on the floor, then you're the luckiest bride this side of the Mississippi. Right?

Takeaway

Your husband is not your problem to fix or project to finish. But if something he does is really irritating, you need to figure out a way to let him know. He really does want you to be happy. The trade-off might be that he'll work hard to change some of his imperfections, if you'll work just as hard to put up with some that cannot be changed.

> *"The Lord works through deeply flawed people, since*
> *He made so few of the other kind."*
> TIMOTHY B. TYSON (1959–)

A Husband Needs His Wife...

To Condone His Man Cave

I don't have a man cave. At least not in the traditional sense.

Frankly, I'm a little jealous of any guy who has one of those classic basement testosterone laboratories featuring leather sofas and recliners, a massive TV, neon logos, posters of leaping running backs, free flowing beverages, and a pantry filled with chips and salsa. If your husband has such a room and lives anywhere in the Chicago area, have him invite me over for the next Bears-Packers game.

All he has to do is dial 630-377-7899 and I'll pick up.

That number rings in the closest thing I have to a man cave. It's my home office, just six steps off the kitchen. The room is the perfect size for pondering, writing, and warehousing my eclectic collection of stuff. Mostly books. Shelves and stacks of books. There's a laptop, printer, phone, and fax machine. A bulletin board with a hundred pushpins puncturing multiple layers of schedules, photos, personal reminders, ideas, and memories. Beneath and behind my desk is a collection of ancient artifacts, including ten-year-old phone books, CDs, cassette tapes, and even some reel-to-reel tapes from my early days as a radio producer. Office and mailing supplies overflow in one corner. Several elementary-school art projects made by kids who are now in their twenties somehow have become part of a permanent exhibit in daddy's office. A smattering of sports equipment, tools that should be on my workbench, once-sacred theater props, and vocal recording equipment fill in any and all gaps. And, yes, I still own a Rolodex.

It's not really a man cave. But it is my sanctuary. And it is a mess. I've long ago given up cleaning it for guests. We just close the door. And I am more than grateful that Rita is okay with that.

You see, Rita likes a clean house. She has a place for everything and she likes everything in its place. For the most part, I agree. More than once in a while, I'll pitch in and vacuum a few rooms, tackle a sinkful of dishes, and wash a few windows. My specialties somehow ended up to be sweeping porches and scrubbing toilets. In more than 30 years of marriage, I think I've done 90 percent of the porch sweeping and 99 percent of the commode scrubbing. But I am no hero.

What I am is grateful. My office/first-floor man cave is a wreck. I admit it. And Rita doesn't rag me about it. When guests are due, she'll gently close the door. In return, I honor her need to have the rest of the house neat and tidy.

Sometimes—especially when I'm preparing to tackle a big project—I'll spend an entire day reorganizing my office and tossing ancient file folders and audio elements, even dusting and wood-polishing. But that happens when I decide, not Rita. When the daylong purge is complete, the room looks significantly better. For about a week.

I'm not sure why Rita puts up with one-tenth of her house lingering in a hopeless state of disarray. Maybe she simply gave up years ago. Maybe she likes the fact that compared to her personal space, my personal space is a disaster. Maybe she is truly appreciative of my willingness to roll up my sleeves and partner with her when the rest of the house needs a lick and a polish. But again, I'm grateful.

If she chose, Rita could focus great amounts of energy on convincing me to clean my office and keep it clean. But the effort would be so draining that other more important segments of her life would suffer. And our relationship would as well.

So I'm glad she doesn't lose sleep over my cluttered office. She knows it's the place I go to write, communicate with the world, think deep thoughts, and generate most of the income that supports our family. Part of me hopes—and trusts—that if the state of my office were suffocating me and preventing me from working productively, Rita would intervene. But she doesn't have to. She knows that the state of my surroundings is not reflected in the state of my output from those surroundings. It's actually an inverse relationship. The documents that leave my office through the magic of the Internet are precise and pristine. I care deeply—perhaps too much—about fonts, margins, page breaks, and readability. I'll lose sleep over a typo that made it past my internal proofreading sentry. Any proposal, script, layout, or manuscript that leaves my cluttered office will be wonderfully uncluttered.

I guess I'm saying this: I need my office to be the way my office is. And there's a good chance that your man needs his man cave to be the way it is. God bless all wives who suppress their justifiable and reasonable rules of logic and let us have our rooms our way.

Takeaway

You need your husband to have a man cave just as much as he needs to have one.

> *"If there hadn't been women we'd still be squatting in a cave eating raw meat, because we made civilization in order to impress our girlfriends."*
>
> —ORSON WELLES (1915–1985)

A Husband Needs His Wife…

To Hold Down the Fort

H as your husband changed career paths or jobs three times since you've been married? Do you wish he would finally figure out what he wants to be when he grows up? Rita and I can relate. It might help if you heard my own long and meandering work history.

I paid for college working as a busboy, bagger, waiter, carpenter, cotton-candy maker, boxcar unloader, and department-store Santa Claus.

Out of college, my first job was selling photocopiers for the A.B. Dick Company. Not Xerox. Not Canon. Not IBM. A.B. Dick. The employee turnover resembled traffic through a revolving door. I lasted two years.

My second full-time job was selling law books to corporate attorneys for Matthew Bender & Company. I was terrible at it. For almost two years I lugged a 26-pound briefcase around Chicago's Loop, finally reinventing myself into a new career just weeks before I was due to be terminated for repeatedly missing my sales quota.

My third job was as a novice copywriter for Menaker & Wright, a tiny ad agency on Chicago's famed Michigan Avenue. They hired me after landing the assignment from Frito Lay to name and position what would become "Sun Chips." When that branding project finished they could no longer afford my minuscule salary. I was let go on my wife's twenty-sixth birthday.

My fourth job was as a copywriter for Campbell-Mithun, a reputable agency with accounts like Midway Airlines, Kroger, and Corona Beer. Over five years, I produced a ton of sparkling work. A new hotshot creative director came in and cleaned house, firing me on my thirty-first birthday, two days after my fourth child was born.

My fifth job was at Domain Communications, a small agency and recording studio in the suburbs that served Christian ministries and publishers. The fit was perfect, but one year later we merged with two other small agencies and the creative department moved to Seattle, leaving me without a full-time job.

My sixth job was not a job at all. For more than 20 years, I have been a freelance writer, producer, author, creativity trainer, speaker, and consultant. Dozens of clients have come and gone. And I only threaten to fire myself a couple of times a year.

While the above résumé seems like it's all about me, I can't reflect on those years without being humbled by a wife who held down the fort at home, and by God who orchestrated every twist and turn.

Men these days are supposed to put their family first. But I must say, to a young dad fighting to find an identity and keep his head above water, that isn't an easy proposition. That's when Rita became my hero. She knew my heart was at home, even when I wasn't. She often held dinner with my young boys until late evening. She fielded nasty phone calls from more than a few bill collectors. She watched the neighbor's kids for a few extra bucks. She knew I was a miserable salesman and she challenged me to chase my dreams. Somehow she knew when to cheer for me and when to scold me. If it weren't for Rita, I'd be living in a van down by the river.

And Rita was just part of God's plan for my life. Looking back, I see his hand in every one of those frustrating jobs and devastating losses. At the time, if you would have quoted the Bible verse that says, "All things God works for the good," I might have strangled you. But now I see that it really is true. I can connect the dots from who I was to who I am. He does work all things for the good. But like so many passages from Scripture, sometimes we forget to read the whole thing. Romans 8:28 actually promises, "In all things God works for the good of those who love him, who have been called according to his purpose."

If your husband is perfectly satisfied in a career that matches his gifts and God's plan, then consider this chapter an entertaining look at this author's bumpy career path. But if you know in your heart that there's something out there better for him, do what Rita did. Hold down the fort at home. Watch your nickels. Stay close. Look for simple joys. Remind your husband of God's love. And challenge him to find God's purpose for his life.

Isn't that why you married him?

Takeaway

Don't be one of those people constantly looking for what's next. Instead, remember to look back so you can see how far you've come and appreciate who was walking beside you every step of the way.

> *"The LORD God said, 'It is not good for the man to be alone. I will make a helper suitable for him.'"*
>
> —GENESIS 2:18

A Husband Needs His Wife...

To Be Careful About Scheduling Expectations

Several years ago, a work colleague sighed deeply and then asked to borrow ten bucks. He had to buy flowers for his wife and was a little short on cash. As I pulled out my wallet, Wally explained that it wasn't a special occasion and he wasn't trying to get out of the doghouse. It was Friday, and every Friday he brought home flowers. He had been doing it for years. My initial thought was, *Oh, that's sweet. I should do that.*

Well, I didn't start that weekly ritual. And thank goodness. Think about what happened the first time Wally brought home flowers. Even if it was just a few daisies or a couple of carnations, his new wife was surprised and delighted. After all, it really is the thought that counts. The next Friday she was delighted again. And the next. I'll even give her credit for being delighted for the first five or six weeks. After that...nothing. The "Friday Flowers" became a laborious, repetitive requirement.

You see, if it really is the thought that counts, then Wally's gift *didn't count!* His only thought was the burden of obligation. There was no joy in the giving or receiving.

Even worse, over the years there was probably a Friday or two on which Wally *didn't* bring home flowers for whatever reason, and I assume those weekends did not get off to a pleasant start. What he had intended as a gift was now a trap.

Perhaps you disagree. Actually, my wife, Rita, likes flowers so much that she might risk saddling me with such an obligation just to have a fresh bouquet on her kitchen table. Full disclosure—I have no personal appreciation for flowers. I recognize and respect Rita's fondness for a nice vase full of fragrant stems, but mostly they just get in the way of my spreading out my morning newspaper.

Just to let you know, I do not buy flowers on any schedule. Although I have become pretty adept at bringing them home once in a while "for no reason." Still, there is no shortage of fresh-cut flowers in our home. My sons and daughter know Mom's weakness for flowers and bring a bunch once in a while. Plus, Rita does not need my permission to buy flowers anytime she feels the need. When I notice them—and frankly sometimes I don't—I will say with just a dollop of sarcasm, "Oh, I see I bought you some flowers." She matches my sarcasm with her own mock appreciation. It's actually a nice give-and-take.

So, like many of the rhythms of our marriage, it took a few years to work out the details. But the flower thing is under control for now.

What about you? What kind of things do you expect, and does your husband know you expect them?

Are there imperatives on your radar screen every day, week, month, or year that are not even a single blip on his? There may be a long list of activities that seem optional to him but are essentials for you: flowers, breakfast in bed, Sunday brunch, watching *Antiques Roadshow* together, a fire in the fireplace, an evening walk around the block, the annual garden show, fireworks on July 4, pizza night, dad tucking the kids in bed, visiting a pumpkin patch, the Christmas tree lighting at Rockefeller Plaza or in your own hometown square.

You may think he knows your every desire and expectation. But he doesn't. Even if you've left clear hints. Even if you've told him flat-out. We forget things and don't pick up on things. Instead of being frustrated because he's not meeting your obvious expectations, help the poor guy out. Give him a hint with a timeline. And be obvious: "Long day today—cuddling up by a fire sounds like heaven." "I'm thinking this is a pizza night!" Or stick the flyer for the pumpkin farm or garden show right on the fridge at eye level.

One thing to keep in mind. From your husband's perspective, some of those activities you're hoping for may not be the best choice. For instance, he knows it's wise to skip fireworks this year because they terrify the new puppy. Your husband might not even consider tucking in the kids because he thinks it is one of your favorite things to do. He realizes you can't stop for brunch after Sunday service because there's a big game that afternoon. If you're going away for the weekend, a bouquet of fresh flowers on Friday evening seems silly, doesn't it?

For sure, much of life requires a schedule. But I believe fresh flowers, breakfast in bed, family bicycle trips to the ice-cream parlor, stargazing, playing Scrabble, and building a snowman should never be written on a calendar too far in advance. Spontaneity is part of the pleasure. Still, at the end of the year, you should be able to see an ongoing pattern of many thoughtful gestures and family moments sprinkled in and through every season. From him to you. And you to him. Some of which are helped along by your gentle reminder or whispered request.

Takeaway

Men do love traditions and making memories. But what we don't love is being told exactly when, where, and how to build traditions and memories. The sudden inspiration and serendipitous discoveries are where the joy comes from.

"When you are older you will understand how precious little things, seemingly of no value in themselves, can be loved and prized above all price when they convey the love and thoughtfulness of a good heart."
—EDWIN BOOTH (1833–1893)

A Husband Needs His Wife...

To Be Captivating

visit my mom every Thursday at the Greenfield Retirement Community. She's in the memory care unit and doing pretty well. Sometimes we have great conversations and sometimes not so much. Sometimes she looks right at me and calls me Kenny. And I'm honored. We lost my dad just a couple of years ago. They were married 60 years.

Margie and Ken's legacy includes four kids and their four spouses. Eleven grandchildren, four of whom are married. Plus four great-grandchildren. That last number we're expecting to increase exponentially in the next decade. For now, that's twenty-seven people who would be stacked below Ken and Margie on the diagram of our family tree.

Consider for a moment what it means to me and those twenty-six other people I love so much that my parents got married, stayed married, and modeled spousal dedication for more than 60 years.

A recent study reveals that children of divorce are roughly twice as likely to see their own marriage end in divorce.[1] Conversely, any marriage that lasts six decades increases the odds of other marriages in the family going the distance. (These are not absolutes, of course, so please don't take anything for granted.)

Here's the point: What my mom and dad did—literally—was to increase the chances that my kids will have long successful marriages.

More specifically, my kids and their kids and their kids have a better chance of avoiding the well-documented devastating negative impact of divorce on families.[2]

- Children of divorced parents are roughly two times more likely to drop out of high school.

- Children of divorce are at a greater risk to experience injury, asthma, headaches, and speech defects.

- Teenagers in single-parent families and in blended families are three times more likely to need psychological help.

- Seventy percent of long-term prison inmates grew up in broken homes.

Again, these are not absolutes. But they do make you consider that there's some value to the concept of staying together for the sake of the kids.

Moving beyond the negative, let's celebrate my parents and millions of other happily married seniors who found young love and made it work. No doubt, they plowed through all kinds of travails and challenges, but the joys far outweighed the struggles. I hope you have a few of those older couples in your family and circles of friends to toast on their golden anniversaries and serve as models for you.

There's a great verse I love to display during my presentations to dads and husbands. I suggest that it might be a good life verse for all men and then click the PowerPoint to reveal Proverbs 5:18-19: "Rejoice in the wife of your youth...let her breasts satisfy you always. May you always be captivated by her love" (NLT). When that verse hits the screen, I can count about three seconds and there's a riffle of chuckling through the room. (Men are really just a bunch of little boys, and that's good to remember.)

Well, it takes me just a moment to get the audience refocused on the core truths of that truth-filled proverb. I tell them, "Men, that girl you married is still that girl you married. Rejoice in her. Be captivated by her love."

So, now I turn to you ladies. What are you doing to inspire your husband to rejoice in you? Are you loving him in a way that is captivating?

It can be done. Margie and Ken Payleitner did it for six decades. Rita and I are halfway there. I wish you the same.

Takeaway

Instead of conjuring up reasons to divorce, spend that same effort looking for reasons to stay married.

"I had a really good childhood up until I was nine, then a classic case of divorce really affected me."
—Kurt Cobain (1967–1994)

A Husband Needs His Wife...

To Let Him Be More Than a Babysitter

I have a friend who babysits his kids. In a conversation, I might ask what he did that afternoon and he'll reply, "I was babysitting the kids." Does that sound like a good dad doing a good thing? Well, it's not.

A dad cannot babysit his own kids. Grandmas, aunts, neighbors, siblings, and nannies can babysit a child. But a dad cannot. Confused? I hope not. Here's the point. When a mom is with her kids, she would never say she's babysitting. She's being a mom. When a dad is with his kids, he can "watch the kids," "spend the afternoon with the kids," or even "be stuck with the kids." But he ain't "babysitting."

Here's another way to think of it. Terms like "babysitting," "housesitting," or "dogsitting" imply that a person is temporarily taking on a role that is not theirs. A babysitting assignment has a beginning and end. Being a parent—a mom or dad—never ends.

All of this wordplay is really just a reminder that—if you have kids of any age—you have a momentous influence on your husband's role as a father. You can set him up for success. Or failure.

If you correct him because he's not holding the newborn properly, he's going to hold the baby less. If you establish yourself as the only person in the world who can get the baby to fall asleep, then your husband is missing out on a chance to connect with his child, and you're missing out on a full parenting partnership with someone who loves that kid as much as you do. If you chastise your husband for playing too rough with the toddler, he is going to feel resentment toward you, and your son or daughter is going to be a weenie. If you argue about parenting choices with your husband in front of your middle-schooler, then you can expect disharmony the next several years as your teenager plays Mom and Dad against each other.

Now, it's entirely possible that you spend more time with your children than your husband does. You may have even taken time off from a well-paying career for the sake of your family. And you are a darn good mom. But that means you have access to insight about your kid(s) that you should be sharing with your husband, not keeping secret from him. By the way, we're jealous of the time you get to spend with the baby or the kids. Plus, our egos are fragile. So when you do have some parenting advice for us, be gentle.

Mommy, if we're not actually damaging the child, then let us hold the baby in a way that's comfortable for us. If you've discovered a secret that works for feeding, burping, or putting the baby down to sleep, share that insider info and let us practice. Give us a weekly rundown of upcoming concerts, games, back-to-school nights, and other can't-miss activities.

By the way, it's really okay if we do stuff with the kids that you wouldn't do. Climbing trees. Playing with snakes. Standing up on a toboggan. Doing cannonballs off the high dive. Taking photocopies of our faces. Seeing how many mini-marshmallows we can catch in our mouth. Waking the kids up in the middle of the night to see a lunar eclipse. That's all mostly dad stuff. (If you ask real nice, we may teach you some of our secrets.)

You know this: Parenting is much easier when Mom and Dad work together. You also know that when there's a disagreement in methodology or strategy, it's best to talk it out in another room. Kids are more secure when Mom and Dad are on the same page.

In all modesty, I need to say that I am a pretty darn good father. Not perfect, but on the right track. And I've had the privilege to share some of my fathering experiences with literally millions of dads via books, TV, radio, and speaking events. But I must confess, it was my kids' mom who set the standard and challenged me to be the father God called me to be.

---------------------- **Takeaway** ----------------------

For whatever reason, maybe you're a little ticked at your husband right now. Sometimes, he might even be a world-class jerk. But I promise you, he wants to be a good father. And those moppets you have living in your house need the best from both of you. A shared goal—such as raising awesome kids—might be the exact thing to get you working together on a mission that must not fail. Just a thought.

> *"Beside every great dad is a great mom."*
> —KEN CANFIELD (1961–)

A Husband Needs His Wife...

To Love On Him

Just about all the conventional wisdom is true. Men like to eat. Men like sports. Men like gadgets. Men like fast cars and monster trucks. Men like movies with chase scenes, explosions, and tough-talking male leads. And, regretfully, men like to look at images of beautiful women with nice curves and enticing smiles. For better or worse, all these things will get our attention.

But we would trade any of those at any moment for a wife who stands, sits, or lies close to us, turns her face toward us, and says, "I love you so much."

Much has been written about the fact that men have a tough time saying "I love you." Women do need to hear those words, don't they? Well, we do too. Actually, men might need to hear it even more because we have fewer intimate relationships. You may be hearing some version of "ILY" from a variety of individuals—children, sisters, parents, and girlfriends.

Sadly, when someone uses the word *love* around your husband, it's usually describing pizza, football, smartphones, or some action flick. But that's not love. And it's certainly not love directed at your husband. That's your job.

So, dear wives, if it's in you...let it out. Say "I love you so much" to your husband tomorrow morning and see if he isn't kinder and sweeter to you and everyone else he meets for the rest of the entire day.

Alternate methods for expressing your love are also very much appreciated. As a public service, here's a convenient list of ways to show us and tell us in ways large and small in the course of the week.

Text him. Leave a sticky note in his briefcase. Leave a cookie wrapped and ribboned on his dashboard. Welcome him home. Smell good for him. Redecorate the bedroom. Invite him to share a bubble bath. Let him control the remote. Buy some massage oil. Use it. Buy him a romantic card when it isn't Valentine's Day.

Cuddle in front of the fireplace. Book reservations at a bed-and-breakfast. At a social gathering, give him a wink or blow him a kiss across the room. Tell him he's your best friend. Tell him he's handsome. Tell him he's a good father. Tell him he's a good lover. Straighten his tie and sneak a kiss. Take him out for Starbucks. Take him out for ice cream. Dance with him in the kitchen—with or without music. Kiss his neck. Bite his earlobe. Jump in the shower with him. Take a walk around the block. Hold hands. Make him breakfast in bed. Bring him some hot coffee when he comes out of the shower. Bring him a cold beverage when he's out mending fences or chopping firewood. Try a new shade of lipstick and ask him to test it. Write him a poem (even one that just starts, "Roses are red...."). Sit on his lap.

There ya go. Words, actions, ideas. Treats. Guaranteed methods for expressing that you really do care for him. He needs this stuff.

But I've saved the best for last. Do you want to know the very best way to "love on" your husband? Here it is. Love on yourself. I know for many of you that's not easy. It's unbelievable how many women look in the mirror and don't like what they see. A favorite author and blogger, Sheila Wray Gregoire, writes,

> Guys, you may look at your wife and think she's beautiful, but I can practically guarantee that she doesn't think so. Everywhere she turns she sees images that she'll never measure up to. And so she feels ugly. And when we women feel ugly, we feel distinctly unsexy...One of the most frustrating things for my husband was when he would proposition me and I would reply, "I just don't feel attractive." His response: "If I want you, you are, by definition, attractive!" He was attracted to me. But I didn't feel attractive.[3]

Can you relate? Do these kinds of thoughts keep you feeling unworthy and unlovable? With your permission, I'd like to take this self-image crisis one step further. Even beyond the marriage relationship.

Because of how women are wired, most of you don't know how wonderful you are. You also don't fully realize how much you are loved by God and by your husband. Well, FYI #1: Your husband would give his life for you. FYI #2: God sent his Son from heaven to give his life for you. If you were the only person on the earth, Jesus loves you so much that he would have sacrificed his life on the cross to pay the penalty for your sins. That's right—you are worth Jesus.

Got it? When you look in the mirror, please see someone who is loved. Let that truth give you new confidence and purpose. And then don't forget to let some of that love overflow toward your deserving husband.

Takeaway

There's a lot packed into the above chapter. Men's needs, women's needs, ideas you can use, and a sincere reminder of God's sacrificial love. Let's end with this thought. It really is pretty easy to show your husband that you love him. You could literally do it in the next three minutes. Will you?

> *"And remember, my sentimental friend, that a heart is not judged by how much you love, but by how much you are loved by others."*
>
> —L. Frank Baum

A Husband Needs His Wife…

To Just Stop It, for Goodness' Sake

I've interacted with and interviewed dozens of wonderful husbands over the last few years. These men are totally devoted to their wives. God-fearing men. Faithful for decades. Loving fathers. Not out drinking, gambling, or other such nonsense. They provide charming dinner-table conversation, appropriate romance, and much or most of the income that pays the mortgage. Upon request they will even carry a flat of daffodils, play a game of Scrabble, or go antiquing.

When I ask about their marriages in general, there is nary a complaint. But when I ask these men specifically to finish the following sentence, they suddenly come up with a short list of items you need to know about.

"I wish my wife would stop…"

The following answers I heard more than once.

"…telling me how to drive." Quite a few men who have relatively clean driving records are being told they're driving too fast, they're taking the wrong roads, and they're approaching a busy intersection. One friend said that he drives 30,000 miles a year on business, but he apparently cannot make it to church without his wonderful and helpful bride suggesting the best route.

"…straightening up the newspapers while I'm still reading them." Hey, we understand you like a neat table. And we know that you like to get a head start on things. And we also know that sometimes we don't always stack the newspapers exactly right. But when I reach over to where I intentionally left the sports section and it's not there, you can understand my frustration.

"…telling me I have food on my face." When a dab of mayo ends up in the corner of one guy's mouth, he hears about it before he can even reach for his napkin. And his bride doesn't let him know with a subtle point to her own

lip. She lets the rest of the table know. It turns out his daughters have picked up the habit, and now he gets ridicule from two generations of his own family. *"…muttering about how I click the TV remote."* Men are natural hunters. We're searching for something better to watch. Or we don't want to waste our lives watching ditzy commercials. Or we sometimes click back a few seconds to hear something we missed. It's not an attack on you, so why do you attack us?

"…correcting minor facts when I'm telling a story." Unless you're in court, it's probably okay if your husband gets a couple inconsequential facts wrong when he's telling an amusing story to a group of friends. If you can add some helpful context or bonus humor to the tale, go for it. Rita and I often tag-team when we tell stories about our kids. But if he says the baseball tournament was in Appleton, and it was actually in Oshkosh, what difference does it make?

I share these above infractions not because they are mortal sins that will destroy healthy marriages. I share them because they are excellent examples of marital glitches you can eliminate this very day.

Did you recognize you and your husband in any of the five examples? In the car? At the breakfast table? Watching TV? At a social gathering? If so, you may want to consider this simple, straightforward request from this husband who cares about your husband: *For goodness' sake, just stop it.* You have that power. You can stop doing that one thing that annoys the man you love so much.

If you didn't see yourself in these examples, don't think you're off the hook. If you have the courage, I challenge you to ask your husband to write down a few ways he might finish that statement. *"I wish my wife would stop…"*

If that exercise turns out to be educational and rewarding, then gently ask your husband if he wants to see your list of things that begin with the phrase, *"I wish my husband would stop…"* He may think this is an ambush, but you can assure him that it comes from a pure heart with no ulterior motives. Then make sure your list isn't too long or too mean-spirited.

By the way, when you compare your two lists, don't be surprised if quite a few items overlap. For instance, you wish he would stop goofing with the remote and he wishes you would stop making such a big deal about it. Hopefully, you can resolve such a dispute without professional counseling.

No matter what, it's good to get these kinds of little irritations and frustrations on the table before they lead to bigger irritations and frustrations—which do, on occasion, require outside help.

Takeaway

It's a good thing wives are around to tell men their faults, otherwise they might never know.

> *"Marriage must incessantly contend with a monster*
> *that devours everything: familiarity."*
> —HONORE DE BALZAC (1799–1850)

A Husband Needs His Wife…

To Be a Great Present-Opener

I am a terrible present-opener. On Christmas morning, I could tear open a package containing a perfect gift chosen carefully just for me by someone I dearly love. It could be something I actually need and truly want and definitely will put to good use. Still, for some reason I don't express the proper enthusiasm or appreciation. It's become a family joke. But it's not really very funny.

Why am I a terrible present-opener? That's an excellent question. Looking back at 30 years of Christmas, birthday, and Father's Day gifts may offer some clues. It could be that my life is already jam-packed and I don't need any more hobbies or distractions. That's why the telescope and hammock left me wondering how and when I would use such devices. It might be that I'm just not a tech guy. That's why I didn't respond with great enthusiasm to the iPod and assorted gifts of software over the years. It might be that I typically opt for comfort rather than style, so my initial reaction to any gift of clothing, footwear, or accessories tends to be quizzical rather than grateful. Sometimes I'll open a gift and think, *That's cool, but when will I use it?* or *Where will I store it?* Gifts from my kids sometimes lead me to think, *That's awesome, but it just cost too much.* Which means my face doesn't reflect my actual appreciation.

Really, I'm not quite that bad. But once you get the reputation as a terrible present-opener, it's hard to shake.

I blame Rita. Because she is the best present-opener in the world. Ask anyone who has ever given her a gift. A niece can give my wife a cheap pair of dime-store earrings and she'll ooh and aah like they came from Cartier. The weekend before Christmas, first-graders would come out of her Sunday-school class absolutely beaming because Teacher Rita swooned over the plate of five cookies or the baggie of chocolate-covered pretzels they had presented to her.

Last Christmas, I bought her a new jewelry box that looked like a beautifully constructed work of art on the company website. But when I opened the UPS package three days before Christmas, I was very disappointed. There wasn't enough time to return it, so I wrapped it expecting her to scowl at the shabby design. Then, after we shared a laugh, I would accompany her on a post-Christmas shopping excursion to find the perfect jewelry box. Instead, she didn't laugh at it. She loved it. Or at least that's what she made me believe. And it's sitting on her bedroom dresser today.

Now you might think that anyone shopping for a gift for Rita would reduce their gift-buying budget. After all, she'll love anything you get her. Instead, they spend *more* time and effort because she is so fun to shop for. I should probably take a hint.

All that to say, I appreciate that Rita shows great appreciation every time for every gift. We've actually established that "Receiving Gifts" is her main love language. If you don't know what that means, I recommend Gary Chapman's book *The Five Love Languages*. He doesn't need a plug from me—I think that book has sold a gazillion copies. Still, if you haven't read it, put down this book and grab that one. It'll change your perspective on relationships. And you will definitely want to figure out your husband's love language.

Worth mentioning is that my love language is "Words of Affirmation." When you put Rita and me together that means it's important for me to give thoughtful gifts to her, and it's equally important for her to affirm my effort in the process. The other three love languages described by Chapman are "Quality Time," "Acts of Service," and "Physical Touch." (It has been suggested that "Physical Touch" is always first or second on the list for husbands, and I can't disagree.)

I know it's not really a big deal when your man brings home a bouquet from the supermarket, makes you a BLT, or spends a Saturday morning with you at an art show. But I encourage you to make it a big deal. If you show some enthusiastic appreciation, he'll do it again. And future gifts and gestures will get bigger and better. Sound like a plan?

─── Takeaway ───

When your husband makes even the smallest gesture of thoughtfulness, choose your response carefully. A guy might have the best intentions, but fail miserably with the execution. If his wife mocks the result, you can understand how he may not make another effort for quite a while.

"There are souls in this world who have the gift of finding joy everywhere, and leaving it behind them when they go."
—FREDERICK WILLIAM FABER (1814–1863)

A Husband Needs His Wife…

To Keep Doing What You're Doing

We don't understand some things you do. But that's okay. We like that you're different from us. That's why we married you.

Personally, there are all kinds of perplexing things Rita does that I have learned to tolerate, accept, or even appreciate. But it has taken me 30 years to come to this enlightened perspective. Your husband may not be experiencing that same kind of understanding or tolerance (and in some cases may never get there). So please be patient.

On behalf of husbands everywhere, I request you spread this simple truth to your sisters, sisters-in-law, girlfriends, and female co-workers. When it comes to many of your habits, personal preferences, and quirks, the men in your lives just don't get it. So please don't expect us to understand. For example:

- Piling decorative pillows on our bed that have to be removed every night and replaced every morning. *And you wonder why a man can never put them back in the proper decorative position.*

- Buying a new purse every six months. *Men can use the same wallet for close to a decade.*

- Being way too nice to another woman you really can't stand and even complimenting her on her outfit and chatting with her like you're old friends. *If a man doesn't like another guy, they both know it and go their separate ways.*

- Never ordering dessert. *But then stealing half of ours.*

- Trying on 14 outfits and ending up wearing the first one you tried on. *Even worse, making us change even though we think we're perfectly presentable.*

- Keeping 34 bottles, spritzers, tubs, tubes, pumps, dispensers, and vials of magic potions on the sink. *On second thought, we like you looking good, so keep doing what you're doing.*

- Saying something is cute. *Men see a puppy and want to teach it to fetch. Men buy a car because of its V-8 or turbocharger. Men carefully examine the features of the new smartphone. Women say, "It's so cute."*

- Asking us, "What are you thinking?" *Do you want us to answer honestly, or should we try to figure out what you want to hear? Either way, we'll probably say the wrong thing.*

- Leaving the gas tank empty. *This is another one of those things that we will gladly do for you. Loading a vehicle with high-octane fuel makes us feel like we're preparing for battle. Just don't ask when we're settling down to watch a championship game or brushing our teeth before bed.*

- Going to the bathroom in packs. *Never mind, we don't want to know what you do in there.*

- Crying. *Except at the death of a pet, winning the Super Bowl (as a participant), visiting Arlington National Cemetery, or hearing "The Star-Spangled Banner," don't expect men to weep along with you.*

Again, these are all things that drive us crazy, but which we have come to totally expect and appreciate. We're glad you're different than us. We're glad you're not one of our male friends. We're glad that we don't have you "figured out." We're glad you do what you do.

Now that doesn't mean we don't like to be surprised once in a while. You know how you kind of like it when your husband shows a softer side? Things like rocking a baby while singing a lullaby, crying when a dog dies in a movie, or gently caring for a baby robin that fell out of its nest? In the same way, husbands sometimes like it when you reveal your slightly more aggressive side. That could include playing touch football with a little extra adrenaline, choosing an action movie over a chick flick, working up a sweat in the garden, or even being a little feistier in the bedroom.

Still, in the end, it comes down to this. You're the girl and we're the boy. For the most part, let's keep it that way. It makes life so much less complicated.

Takeaway

Men are not better than women, just as women are not better than men. They're just different. And thank God.

> *"Remember, Ginger Rogers did everything Fred Astaire did, but she did it backwards and in high heels."*
>
> —FAITH WHITTLESEY (1939–)

A Husband Needs His Wife...

To Give Him Time to Decompress After Work

My son Randall and his bride, Rachel, have a great marriage. As proof, I offer this story. It may sound too good to be true, but I assure you every word is indeed unimpeachable.

Randall works at a book-publishing house in downtown Chicago as an associate publisher. Rachel is an interior designer for a global architectural firm with an office on the thirty-sixth floor overlooking the Chicago River. For four years, they have coordinated their schedules on most days to leave home in the morning and leave their offices in the evening so they can commute together.

When they were living in their apartment in Logan Square, and later in Old Irving, they would fight traffic somewhere between 20 and 40 minutes to and from their River North offices. In his faithful Saab, Randall gave curbside service to his bride in the morning and then drove the ten blocks to the parking garage at his own building. Around 5 p.m., a phone call or a few quick text messages would confirm a timely connection at the end of the workday. And that's where our application for wives and husbands begins.

Like most gals, Rachel would slip into the passenger seat, kiss her handsome husband, and begin to share the ups and downs of her day. Not surprisingly, Randall listened dutifully. After all, he truly cared about everything she was saying and wanted to give his bride encouragement, advice, and support. It was all good. Except for one problem. After finishing his own workday, he just wasn't ready for that kind of interaction.

Like most guys, Randall needed to decompress. In silence. Or with the radio on in the background—music, talk, news, sports, whatever. And it turns out the ten-block drive from his office to hers wasn't long enough. He wanted—no, he needed—another ten minutes or so.

Clearly, the stage was set for a major confrontation.

But that never happened. Call it women's intuition. Call it being perceptive. Call it being in tune to the needs of your husband, but Rachel somehow discerned what was going on during the first few miles of their homebound commute. Her husband had not complained or showed overt signs of frustration, but neither was he fully engaged.

Truth be told, Randall didn't know what he needed. But Rachel did. She made a suggestion and it worked.

For the next couple of years, the commuting schedule didn't change much. But the communication pattern did. Rachel jumped into the car and kissed her husband, and the couple would take just a moment to cover any details necessary for the first part of the drive home: *"The Cubs game is just finishing so the Kennedy is going to be jammed." "We need to stop at Walgreen's on the way." "I noticed the right front tire is low."* And the evening would begin in quiet. Even the noise of the traffic would fade into the background.

Then not too much later—five or ten minutes—Randall or sometimes Rachel would break the silence with an anecdote worth sharing or a reminder of plans for the evening: *"I just got the new manuscript I've been expecting. It's real good." "I'm exhausted, but looking forward to Bryan and Katie coming over tonight." "You know, Randy, I'm thinking you have the best dad in the world."*

The truths woven into this story are clear: Women need to talk about their day. Men need time to decompress from theirs. Conflict in marriage may be avoided by choosing to discern each other's needs.

Also, this thought comes to mind. Next time you pull up beside a car in which a husband and wife are staring straight ahead in obvious silence, don't immediately assume they have a terrible, noncommunicative marriage. It could be she is giving him the great gift of 15 minutes of post-workday decompression. In return, he will surely give her his full attention when the time is right.

Randall and Rachel's story doesn't end there. Last summer, they bought a house in the suburbs within walking distance of the commuter train depot. They still leave home in the morning together for the ride into the city. But in the evening they don't meet in front of Rachel's building. They rendezvous right on the train. Usually the 5:09. Usually in the designated *quiet* car.

Which means the two wordlessly kiss hello and contently sit in silence for 34 minutes. They might read, listen to their iPods, or take turns napping on each other's shoulders.

A half hour later, they detrain at their hometown station. My son tells me the two of them typically hold hands for the walk home, quite ready to chit-chat and catch up on their day and their lives.

Takeaway

By taking time to quiet your hearts, both you and your husband will get the most out of your time together. It removes distractions, allowing you to give full attention to each other. Prayer works the same way. Psalm 46:10 reminds us that the best way to find God is with less noise and more reflection: "Be still, and know that I am God."

"A properly kept silence is a beautiful thing; it is nothing less than the father of very wise thoughts."

—Diodicus

A Husband Needs His Wife...

To Be Flattered When You're on His Mind

This chapter is where the author fully acknowledges he doesn't know everything about women. Although that should already be painfully obvious. How women operate—what a woman wants—is one of the great unanswerable questions of all times. Entire books have been written on the topic. Movies, talk shows, and stadiums filled with men have focused on discerning the answer to that exact question, only to come up with glib, unproven, or halfbaked hypotheses.

Case in point. During the course of a particular workday your husband is so focused on a challenging task that he barely thinks about you or your family. That seems ironic. And he actually feels a little guilty. The primary reason he's working is to love and support his family, so shouldn't you always be top of mind?

The following week, he pauses and smiles 20 times during the course of a workday because you do come to mind. He's not even sure why, but a scene flashes through his mind of your courtship, he imagines you in that old grey sweatshirt with the paint spots, he recalls the exact words of a conversation the two of you had three years ago at Starbucks, he spends a moment plotting the schedule for this coming weekend, and for no reason at all he pulls out his phone and flips through a dozen photos of you. Really, some days husbands do all those things. That's good, right?

Then later that day your husband says something that seems wonderfully innocent, but you take it entirely the wrong way: "I was thinking about you all day today."

Your reaction? *Oh gee! Here it comes. I'm exhausted. Plus, I'm getting that flu bug that's going around work. I've got a jillion things going on in my head including bills, laundry, that stupid picnic on Saturday, and the leaking dishwasher. And he's been thinking about me all day. What makes him think* that *is good news?*

Admittedly, he's testing the water. He's hoping your response is something like "Thanks, Sweetheart. I've been thinking about you too!" That indicates to your husband there's a greater than average chance that there will be some serious romance happening in the next 72 hours. Maybe even tonight.

On the other hand, he actually expects your response to be lukewarm. He expects a roadblock because that's your typical response. Even when there's no car on the road, the barriers still go up with stunning efficiency. What happens when that happens? Suddenly the room turns from lukewarm to ice-cold. He excuses himself to go check his e-mail and you don't see him for the rest of the evening. You're left wondering what happened. And he's left a little sadder and a little frosted.

It didn't have to unfold this way. Two people who love each other and are committed to each other for life should be able to hold a nice conversation—beginning to end—and come out smiling. Can I put this challenge in your lap? After all, he didn't do anything wrong. He was just saying "hi."

Let's rewind the tape...

He says: "I was thinking about you all day today."

You say: "Really—you were thinking about me? Like what?"

Suddenly you've launched a nice little conversation—silly, serious, profound, or otherwise. It may go for a mere 30 seconds, or it may last all through dinner. Isn't that nicer than frostbite city? For no extra charge, allow me to suggest a wonderful way to end that conversation. You say: "Tell you what, you keep thinking about me and I'll keep thinking about you. And just maybe sometime in the next few days (or maybe this weekend) we can turn those thoughts into action. How does that sound?"

Do you see how that works? Do you see what you did there? You pulled him into your world and accomplished about six different things. 1) You had a nice conversation. 2) You heard a little about his day. 3) You satisfied his need to connect to you. 4) You scheduled sex—not for tonight—but for some time later that week. 5) You freed up the rest of your night for your extensive to-do list. 6) And you've given him all-new reasons to think about you for the next few days.

Your last assignment is to remember your date sometime before the weekend ends. If you can drop some other thought-provoking hints in the meantime and come up with an idea or two to make the evening even more special, then you are a mile ahead of most of the other wives reading this chapter. But of course, it's not a competition. Or is it?

Takeaway

Your husband is not your enemy. Next time you feel the need to push him away, instead pull him closer and put a nice firm date on the calendar.

> *"You know what charm is: a way of getting the answer yes without having asked any clear question."*
> —ALBERT CAMUS (1913–1960)

A Husband Needs His Wife…

To Keep the Light On for Him

I s this joke funny? I think guys get it and gals might not.

> *NEWS FLASH: Friday evening. A notorious murderer has just escaped from Texas State Prison. Police advise members of the public they should not approach him at any cost, but report any sightings to their nearest police station.*
>
> *NEWS FLASH: Saturday afternoon. The convict who escaped from Texas State Prison late Friday evening is safely back in custody after surrendering himself to police early this morning.*
>
> *When asked why he gave himself up after his first taste of freedom in 12 years, the man replied, "When I finally got home, the first thing my wife asked me was, 'Where have you been? You escaped eight hours ago.'"*[4]

You need to know that sometimes that's how you make your husband feel. He comes in the door and you jump all over him because he's 27 minutes later than usual. That's not a fun way to start your evening. That's not a fun way to live your life. At the very least, please give him a chance to explain.

He may have the best excuse in the world. He may have been forced to finish a project for a demanding boss. He may have been consoling a work colleague whose son is in rehab. He may have been at the jewelry store picking out the perfect stones for your anniversary ring.

Should he have called? Yes. Did he try to call and couldn't? Maybe. Here's the sequence of events that happens more times than you realize. He's running late for whatever reason. He's distracted by real things that matter enormously

but are hard to explain. Deadlines. Cash flow. Work conflicts. Personnel problems. Many times the priorities and vexations crashing around his head are
all about how he can be a better husband.

He knows he's late. He has already told himself to call you as soon as he
gets off the elevator. Or when the traffic clears. Or after he sends that text to
the incompetent supplier in Kansas who missed another shipment. Three
more crises interrupt his train of thought. And by then it's too late to call.
He begins some wishful thinking. No man wants to call home and say, "I'm
going to be late," when he's already late.

Instead, he hopes for the best and slips in the front door, praying that
you're distracted, napping, in a great mood, or out running errands.

What he's really hoping is that his wonderful, devoted wife greets him at
the front door with a kiss and cold beverage like a conquering hero should
be welcomed at the end of a tough day of battle. But what are the chances of
that happening?

Wives, can you help us out in this area?

First, please know that you are better at phoning, staying in touch, and
anticipating delays than we are. In our quest to gets things done, we become
focused with laser intensity on one task and then move to the next task without looking at our watch or thinking about where we need to be four tasks
from now. I'm not making excuses. (Actually, I guess I am.) But quite often
time slips by and we end up in scramble mode.

Second, if there is really something critical that evening—a band concert,
couples' group, a meeting with a teacher—help us remember. With today's
technology, there are all kinds of alarms, messages, texts, and calendar beeps
that do a better job than tying a string around your husband's finger.

Third, don't "test us" to see if we remember. Because if we fail that test,
everyone loses. If you do find yourself saying, "I knew you'd forget," then
maybe some of the fault is yours. If you really did know, then you should
have done whatever it takes to remind us.

Fourth, if you do remind us seven times, don't be surprised if we snap
back with "I know, you told me already!" If that happens, you can escalate
the anger by saying, "Well, I have to say everything ten times because you
never listen and you always forget!" Or you can temper your response with a
quieter, gentler approach: "Well, this is important to Beth, and I know how
busy your schedule is." Like all arguments, we make choices to stoke the fire
or turn the heat down. When possible, always choose the latter.

Fifth, when your husband does say he is sorry for being late, accept his apology. His tone may not sound sincere, but he is more frustrated with the situation than you are. Really.

The irony is that all the anger and frustration is caused by the fact that you both want the same thing. You want him home and he wants to be home. And home should be a place of comfort, respite, and even reprieve. Another word that comes to mind when we think of home is "grace." Whenever you extend grace to your husband, you both win.

All that to say, if you're glad he's home, let him know.

Takeaway

You may not want to frame a needlepoint of Proverbs 15:1 for your family room, but it's a verse all family members should remember. "A gentle answer turns away wrath, but a harsh word stirs up anger." And don't just breeze past those two options. Day after day, conversation after conversation, there are almost always two ways to respond—with a gentle answer or a harsh word. Your choice.

"Let the wife make the husband glad to come home, and
let him make her sorry to see him leave."

—Martin Luther (1483–1546)

A Husband Needs His Wife…

To Cry and Laugh Together with Him

It would be logical to assume that most of your major arguments happen when you and your husband are both having bad days. Frustrations and disappointments simmer for hours and finally explode when you are in each other's company. You've both trained yourselves not to throw tantrums at work, in public, at church, with the kids, or in front of the neighbors. But with your spouse, sometimes it just feels right to let loose. "We were both having a bad day" is also a convenient excuse for irascible behavior.

But I submit the biggest husband-wife arguments that leave the deepest scars occur when one of you is having a no-good, terrible rotten day and the other is having just the opposite.

Think about it. All week he's looking forward to Saturday where he gets to do his thing—fishing, golf, hunting, Civil War reenactment, a car show, softball, tailgating at his alma mater's football game. You even wish him well because you know he'll have fun. And he does.

You were also looking forward to that same Saturday, but every part of the day you imagined crumbles or backfires. You can't find your good jeans, and the top you wanted to wear has an unidentified green stain on the sleeve. The friend you were meeting at Panera cancels because of a sick kid. A clerk is rude, gas has gone up 12 cents, the trick for fixing your iPhone glitch that always works doesn't work anymore, and the amazing craft store worth the 45-minute drive from home has gone out of business. Which you discover in their parking lot. You pull in the driveway the same time as your husband. His big smile just ticks you off even more.

It works the other way too. On an arbitrary weekday, your hair looks great. Your nails look great. It's a skinny day. You dominate in two meetings and personally close the deal with a new client, thereby preventing multiple layoffs next quarter. You feel empowered and worthy for the first time in a long time. It's a great day. Much to the contrary, his ego has spent the last ten hours being dragged through the mud.

Wouldn't it be wonderful if the spouse experiencing a good day could elevate the spouse experiencing the bad day? It typically doesn't work that way. Instead, Mr. Frustrated or Mrs. Grouchy goes on the attack, intentionally accusing the other party of a lack of understanding or compassion. No one really communicates. Sniping remarks whiz right past each member of the dueling couple. When the volume finally dies down, he and she are both left wondering if they married the wrong person.

Did you ever feel that way? Extreme emotions leading to more extreme emotions.

One of my favorite Bible verses delivers clear instructions for these times. It's Romans 12:15. Read it and then say it out loud. "Rejoice with those who rejoice; mourn with those who mourn." It doesn't matter who is smart enough to put this advice into action. But the idea is to make a conscious choice to match your spouse's emotions.

If he's having a cruddy day—because you love him and care about him—you will pick up on those signals fairly quickly. "Sweetheart, I'm so sorry," or "Pookie, come get a hug from your Cuddle Bunny," are much nicer things to say than, "You had a bad day! I get it! But don't drag me down with you."

If he had a tremendous day but you're still steaming, it would be nice if he matched your emotions and mourned right alongside you. But if that doesn't happen, challenge yourself to take a step back, evaluate the situation, and choose to follow the instructions of Romans 12 and rejoice with him.

What shouldn't happen is that you take your Top Ten Day and his Zero Day and average them out. Living with mediocre days is no fun at all. I would much rather cry with Rita or laugh with Rita than just exist in denial of our emotions.

Takeaway

Romans 12:15 works at all times with all emotionally charged situations. When you enter a circumstance where someone is celebrating or hurting, join them in that moment. Set aside your own agenda or needs for now. "Rejoice with those who rejoice; mourn with those who mourn." It doesn't have to last for hours. When the time is right, you'll know when it's time to introduce a different set of emotions or expectations to the relationship.

> *"Don't take the wrong side of an argument just because your opponent has taken the right side."*
>
> —Baltasar Gracián (1601–1658)

A Husband Needs His Wife…

To Forgive Him, Especially If He Won't Forgive Himself

In the year 2000, my friend Cameron lost virtually everything he and his wife owned in the stock market. It happened very fast. They had just sold their business and he had reinvested every nickel into stock options when the market peaked…and crashed. At one point, he recalls losing more than $30,000 a day for several days in a row. When the last of his options hit bottom, there was no cash value left to give hope for any kind of recovery. The fault was his. He accepted that. The guilt was immeasurable.

Worst of all, he would have to break the news to his wife.

Maggie trusted him. She had watched him work hard over the first 20 years of their marriage. She had partnered with him in almost every key decision about careers, life goals, where to live, how to raise the kids, and even investing for retirement. She had no reason not to trust him. He was a good man with good values and good decision-making skills.

Maybe he got greedy. Maybe he took some bad advice. Maybe he just had a streak of bad luck. Or maybe God was trying to teach him something. In God's sure timing, the reason Cameron got burnt by the stock market may even have been so that he could tell me this story…so I could tell it to you.

In any case, some prideful men have been known to keep that kind of life-shattering secret for months or years. Denial is a tempting accomplice in these situations. But Cameron came clean. In his heart, he knew approaching his wife with honesty and humility was his only option. He wasn't sure how Maggie would react. They had a solid marriage, but when ravaged by a financial crisis, many similar marriages end in a divorce.

Cameron remembers specific quotes from that day. *"All of it. Honey, it's all gone." "How could you let this happen?" "I'm so, so sorry."* But even hearing desperate words of contrition, she could not forgive him. At least not right away. It's not that Maggie was angry, but she had so much to process. So much to think through. The feeling of violation and lost trust was undeniable.

Cameron doesn't tell the story often. The memories are held in check, still too painful. But he is quite clear about the unspoken decisions by wife and husband that kept their marriage from breaking. They didn't raise their voices. She didn't rub his face in it. They talked. They listened. They faced the painful reality and together picked up the pieces.

She could have stabbed him over and over with blame. And the blood would still be flowing. He could have turned the entire episode on her. After all, wasn't he was only trying to provide for her needs? Instead they forgave. Especially Maggie. Today, Cameron speaks in glowing terms about his bride. "She was remarkable. She *is* remarkable."

With a hint of gratitude in his voice, Cameron says his marriage and faith are stronger now because of the brokenness they endured together. He won't say that it was a good thing. But as a medical professional he confirms, "When a bone breaks, it heals stronger."

He won't let the story be told without quoting Colossians 3:13: "Forgive as the Lord forgave you." That's worth remembering.

But for our purposes, let's further examine that verse in context. Writing from prison, Paul is instructing all believers in how to live with each other. If we draw out a few more verses, I think you'll agree these powerful 70 words paint an enduring image of love, respect, and mutual surrender for marriage:

> Clothe yourselves with compassion, kindness, humility, gentleness and patience. Bear with each other and forgive one another if any of you has a grievance against someone. Forgive as the Lord forgave you. And over all these virtues put on love, which binds them all together in perfect unity. Let the peace of Christ rule in your hearts, since as members of one body you were called to peace. And be thankful (Colossians 3:12-15).

Thanks, Cameron. You've given us much to think about. Forgiveness. Communication. Perseverance. Humility. And also why we shouldn't risk our entire nest egg in the stock market.

Takeaway

Up for a challenge? Especially if you're facing a crisis or dry spell in your marriage (or even if you're not), grab your Bible and your sweetheart and take turns reading all four chapters of the book of Colossians. It's about 2200 words. It will take you about 12 minutes to read aloud. You'll be amazed at how the life principles Paul proposed in the first century still work so well in the twenty-first.

"Peace I leave with you; my peace I give you. I do not give to you as the world gives. Do not let your hearts be troubled and do not be afraid."

—JOHN 14:27

A Husband Needs His Wife…

To Not Join In on the Husband-Bashing

You can imagine the scene. Maybe you've been a part of the scene. Between three and ten women sitting in a living room, restaurant, or community center trash-talking their husbands or ex-husbands. It may be a work outing. It may be a new-mom support group. It may be a booster club planning some fundraising event and all the volunteers happen to be women. It may even be a women's Bible study.

One woman innocently makes a joke. Another makes a slightly meaner joke. And pretty soon the entire conversation drags down everyone in the room, their husbands, and their marriages. The community too, for that matter.

Years ago, my wife was part of a biweekly gathering of homemakers who brought their sewing, needlepoint, and knitting projects. Please excuse the expression, but they literally called it "Stitch and Bitch." Funny? Perhaps. Uplifting? Not at all.

As you're reading this, there are probably two or three women who come to mind who are always ready to start the negative chatter. I'm not sure why they are so miserable. But I'm assuming they have also left a trail of husbands (or ex-husbands) who are also miserable.

If you find yourself in an ongoing vortex of bitterness, how should you respond? If you feel compelled to join in, please don't. And excuse yourself from other such meetings with that group. But if you feel empowered by your relationship with your husband and confident that your voice will be heard, could you do all of us guys a favor? Find the right words to deflect the bashing, or at least give the group something to think about.

"There's such a negative vibe going on here—especially against husbands—is that really necessary?"

"Let's change the direction of this conversation—what do you think?"

"I'm not sure where this is all coming from, but men are not the enemy."

"I have to say, you're starting to make me really appreciate my husband."

Your goal is not to paint yourself as a saint or suggest your husband is perfect. And it's quite possible all that husband-bashing is really just a cry for help. The best answer might not be to confront the worst culprit in the large-group setting, but rather talk to her one on one after your meeting. A simple "Are you okay?" might be exactly what she needs to hear and may even open the door to some counseling or an invitation to your church or a study group with a better attitude.

Any intervention you attempt may not change the heart of the most vocal offenders. But you might prevent collateral damage among the other women in the group. There may be some younger participants who have not built up any immunity to the rampant spread of man-hating poison. If you can prevent one or two from becoming infected, you may save a marriage or deter a young bride from picking a fight with her unsuspecting husband later that evening.

I've never attended an all-women's meeting, but my sources tell me that husband-bashing is quite contagious. Immunize yourself with good thoughts and a new appreciation for your own man. Protect others with a pro-marriage comment or quip. And see if you can't stop the infection at its source.

Oh yeah, here's one more strategic line you might want to try:

"You know, I happen to be reading this not-too-painful book for wives. It's 52 short chapters, and I just finished chapter 18. I'd be happy to lend you my copy when I'm through."

Takeaway

Husband-bashing is another example of a self-fulfilling prophecy. Trash-talk your man and you'll begin to treat him like garbage. His only choice will be to start smelling and going bad.

> *"Do not let any unwholesome talk come out of your mouths,*
> *but only what is helpful for building others up according*
> *to their needs, that it may benefit those who listen."*
> —EPHESIANS 4:29

A Husband Needs His Wife…

To Redeem Those Love Coupons Promptly

Has your husband ever given you a booklet of love coupons? Did you cash them in? What are you waiting for?

If you don't know what we're talking about, you haven't been exploring your share of kitschy knickknack stores or browsing beyond the traditional bookshelves of your favorite bookstore. Love coupons are typically check-sized booklets of certificates that can be redeemed for romantic or thoughtful activities at some future date. The concept only works if the receiver takes the gift seriously and actually tears off a coupon and expectantly hands it back to the giver. No spoken words are required, which is part of the beauty of love coupons. Still, my extensive, completely made-up research reveals that of the 12.4 million preprinted love coupons presented from a husband to a wife, only seven have been redeemed.

What inspired this love-coupon boom? Years ago, some clever and hopelessly romantic dude very likely created a bundle of handwritten coupons that had significant personal meaning to a young lady with whom he was smitten. Something like "This certificate redeemable for one Italian ice at Giuseppe's on Main Street on a hot summer day." Cashing in that coupon would be a no-brainer. Other easy-to-redeem custom love coupons might have been something like "A rowboat ride for two on the Central Park lagoon" or "Sunday brunch with Karyn and Tom." The heartfelt love-coupon idea was well received and the couple told other couples who told other couples, and so on.

Seeing the profit potential, gift-book publishers and greeting-card companies picked up on the concept. The first round of professionally designed and printed love coupons was fairly tame and innocent. Then—as happens with most cultural trends—the selfish side of human nature revealed itself. Suddenly, the coupons became a gift for the giver. Even worse, the lovely idea has become another instance for husbands and wives to miscommunicate and feel guilty about not meeting each other's expectations.

Still, let's not throw out the entire concept. Approached with the right attitude, love coupons can be a pleasant diversion, a selfless gift, or even a learning experience. If you take the time to really read through them, you'd find some of them quite desirable and even practical:

Redeemable for breakfast in bed.

One-hour bubble bath without interruption.

One morning of sleeping in late with no responsibilities of feeding any pets or caring for any children.

Good for one late-night run to satisfy a craving for ice cream, french fries, Mexican food, Chinese food, a caramel macchiato, or any other taste not available in our kitchen.

Any three household chores completed efficiently without complaint.

Good for one kiss-and-make-up. Argument over. No questions asked.

Coupons like that are worth a second look. They are true sacrificial gifts with no strings attached, and any woman would be wise to take full advantage of such offers. Other coupons worth redeeming are designed to bring you a generous supply of personal enjoyment and just might deliver a smaller dose to your husband as well:

One evening of dinner and dancing.

Movie night: At home or the theater. You pick the flick.

A self-guided walking tour of where we met, first kissed, and fell in love.

An evening of cuddling and kissing...just cuddling and kissing.

Which brings us to the kinds of coupons that understandably are often left in the bottom of your dresser drawer. These are the love coupons that few women would have the courage to tear off and redeem. And the giver is left wondering why:

Good for one full body massage.

Good for one romantic candlelit bath for two.

Good for one "quickie" anytime and anyplace.

Please don't be offended by such suggestions. We're just throwing out options and letting you know that we're here for you. You are the focus of our attention. You represent the deepest desires of our heart. Nothing pleases us more than when we get a chance to please you. That includes rowing you across a lagoon or massaging your feet after a hard day at work. Honestly—coupon or not—just tell us what you want. If a silly preprinted certificate gives you the incentive to make a request, then we both win.

Worth noting: Many of the love coupon booklets include a wild and wide range of offers involving skinny-dipping, whipped cream, and other questionable proposals. We're not going there. We want to stay in your comfort zone. It's your total call.

The final word on this matter is this. If your husband gives you a stack of love coupons, don't read too much into it or overanalyze his motivations. But do flip through them. Chuckle at some. Raise your eyebrows at a few. Say, "Oh, I don't think so," to a couple of them.

And make a mental note of those specific coupons you intend to redeem sometime in the next couple of weeks.

Takeaway

If you've never received a gift of love coupons from your husband, then you now know the perfect gift to give to him on your next anniversary, Valentine's Day, or just because.

*"It doesn't matter what you do in the bedroom, as long as
you don't do it in the street and frighten the horses."*
—Mrs. Patrick Campbell (1865–1940)

A Husband Needs His Wife…

To Put In Your 10,000 Hours

If you want a scientifically inspired plan to stick with your husband, then stick with this chapter for a few paragraphs while we sift through a recent sociological theory that may apply to your marriage.

You may have heard of Malcolm Gladwell. A writer for the *New Yorker*, his bestselling books include *The Tipping Point*, *Blink*, and *Outliers*. In *Outliers*, Gladwell presents some research done by the psychologist Anders Ericsson, adding some of his own spin along the way. He calls it the "10,000 Hour Rule," which suggests that achieving greatness in virtually any endeavor requires you or your team to invest that many hours of your life.

To prove his point, Gladwell provides thought-provoking examples. From 1960 to 1963, the Beatles played 1200 eight-hour shows in Hamburg, Germany. (That's 9600 hours.) By the time they returned to England, they had found their unique sound. When they landed at JFK in New York City in February 1964 and appeared on the *Ed Sullivan Show*, the Beatles were mistakenly considered by many to be an "overnight success."

Another example takes us to Seattle in 1968. Then-13-year-old Bill Gates is given rare access to a high-school computer and spends 10,000 hours developing his programming skills. One more case in point—a college-age violin virtuoso has typically practiced two hours per day since kindergarten.

So what does that have to do with your marriage? Well, some of you already know where this is going. But let's do the math anyway.

Using Gladwell's rule, it takes 10,000 hours to achieve greatness as a spouse. While dating, guys and gals are projecting false identities, right? During your engagement, it's all about prepping for the big day. So you really can't begin practicing the art and science of marriage until after the honeymoon.

At 24 hours a day, you could be a great spouse in just 416.6 days. But really, you're not practicing your marriage skills round the clock. As a matter of fact, I submit that most husbands and wives spend—at most—about an hour a day interacting and working out the details of life as a couple. Hmm. That's one hour per day for 10,000 days. Or 27 years.

So how long have you been married? When Rita and I hit our twenty-seventh year, our kids were becoming more independent and didn't need our constant attention. At the same time, the two of us were settling into a new appreciation for each other's gifts, strengths, and shortcomings. During that transitional season, I distinctly remember a new feeling of contentment. We had not stopped learning and growing. We weren't giving up or retiring. We were not entrenched in a mind-numbing routine. Nor were we frolicking in continuous delirious waves of bliss. There was a very real sense that we had reached a kind of marital tipping point. We were simultaneously making a mutual discovery that our life together made sense. It was a contentment that only comes from experience and partnership. By our twenty-seventh anniversary we knew that, between the two of us, there was nothing we couldn't handle. We trusted God. We trusted each other. We even trusted that any disagreements would not pull us apart, but actually bring us closer together.

If you're engaged or just married, this chapter won't make sense. You'll just have to trust me. If you're enduring the "seven-year itch," I totally understand. You're thinking this marriage deal should be paying dividends by now, and your husband is still doing things that confuse you or tick you off. But I urge you to be patient. After all, you're really only one-quarter of the way there.

Consider any photos taken at a magical silver wedding anniversary gala. They may reveal sincere smiles, but also a stunning question mark over the head of both the guests of honor. *Is this all there is? I've invested a quarter-century in this guy and he still doesn't understand my need for (fill-in-the-blank)? Who is that middle-aged gal standing next to that middle-aged guy?*

Then a few years later that couple hits the 10,000-hour mark and it all makes sense. Contentment. Purpose found. Deep impenetrable love as designed by the One who created marriage in the first place.

It's all just a theory, mind you. But like all good theories it has some corollaries and exceptions:

- Hours spent living together before marriage don't count.
- Get divorced before 10,000 hours and you have to start all over again.

- Couples earn triple credit for all hours spent at the hospital taking care of each other or looking after really sick kids.

- Wives get a 500-hour bonus for reading this book. And your husband earns full credit if you apply any of these 52 principles.

My publisher tells me that all kinds of women will be reading these words. Different circumstances, needs, expectations, ages, and stages. If you're just getting started, please don't be overwhelmed by the idea that you have to wait 27 years before finding love. The truth is, you'll very likely be so busy living life that you'll get there faster than you can imagine. And, if you're well beyond 30 years of marriage and you're still waiting for that sense of contentment and purpose, I urge you to stop and look around. I'll bet it's already there.

Ultimately, I hope this chapter speaks to those wives (and husbands) who are in those mid-range years still learning the ups and downs of married life and sometimes looking past each other for answers. I invite you instead to look at each other. Look to the life partner God has given to you. The more time you invest in each other, the more likely you are to discover the answers to your deepest questions, and the more likely you are to uncover all the best life has to offer—today, tomorrow, and forever.

Takeaway

I wish for you greatness in your marriage. Even if it takes a few years.

"Love seems the swiftest but it is the slowest of all growths.
No man or woman really knows what perfect love is
until they have been married a quarter century."
—MARK TWAIN (1835–1910)

A Husband Needs His Wife...

To Rescue Him from Himself

Your husband has two kinds of flaws. The ones that bother you. And the ones that bother others.

As for the former, I hope you have chosen a plan of action. Either accepting them or easing him away from his nasty habits and shortcomings that get under your skin. Just for reading this book, I believe you deserve a new and improved husband.

As for the latter kind of flaws, you have a responsibility there as well. In many ways, the bothersome habits your husband inflicts on outsiders are much more critical. For one thing, he doesn't have a lifelong commitment to the rest of the world, so they can abandon him on a whim. And for another, his bad habits that irritate others may result in a punch in the face or a police record. They can also lead to lost friends, lost jobs, lost respect, and lost ministry opportunities. As his faithful wife, you may be called to take extreme measures to rescue the man you love from his own destructive behaviors.

My most serious flaw has not led to any jail time or broken noses. But it's led to some personal losses that I regret to this day. You see—I confess—I am the jerk in the stands. Before you judge too harshly, let me explain. Before the game, after the game, during 96 percent of the game, I'm a delightful companion offering sparkling conversation and witty commentary on the decisions by the coaches and the calls by the officials. But much to my dismay, a few times during every season—watching my kids participate in a sport—I would speak, mutter, or yell things that were way out of line.

Actually, I have learned to tone it down over the years. Still, I can't bear to think of the occasions when members of my own family were regretting I was there. In my head I can replay images of how I acted, and it's more than a little frustrating. It's almost like an out-of-body experience. I ask myself, *Who is this guy? Why is he making such a fool of himself?*

To be clear, I didn't yell negative words at my kids or any of the young athletes. It was mostly at refs. Sometimes at the situation. Often it was just over-the-top-loud game analysis. Frustration boiling over. Many times I would aggressively voice what many of the other fans were thinking. That's when my wife would tell me, "Jay, your voice carries" or, "Jay, I think the other dads would love to stand with you way down the third-base line." Which I hated to hear, but I needed to hear.

Which, of course, is the point. When your husband screws up, he may need your help. The challenge is that—even if we're about to hurtle over a cliff—most men don't want to be corrected by our wives. That tends to make matters go from bad to worse. If I'm a jerk and Rita calls me on it, I often respond by being even more of a jerk. Still, it's the right thing for her to do.

Other examples. If a husband is rude to a waiter or clerk, we want our wife to let us know. If our body odor is nasty, we want you to tell us. If we're about to park in a tow zone or on the neighbor's grass, say something. If your husband is about to track mud into his boss's house, is talking too loudly on his cell phone, or is holding up a long line at a ticket counter for a measly three bucks, he wants you to gently point out how his action could be improved. It may not be pleasant to hear, but that's part of your job and you need to have the courage to do it.

Ideally, a husband eventually recognizes his flaw and actually requests his wife's intervention. But don't hold your breath. The best you can hope for is that on the car ride home, he delivers some sort of apology or regret which gives you a chance to gently offer to help. If you respond, "Heck yeah, you were an absolute embarrassing jerk," that's not going to help. What will help is for you to come alongside and let him know that he is otherwise the perfect man of your dreams but he does have one teensy-tiny flaw. Good luck with that.

Over the years, Rita and I have tried a variety of strategies to minimize my jerk-in-the-stand scenarios. We've talked about it. We've prayed about it. I've given her permission to nudge me if I start acting up. I've learned to walk down to the foul pole or end zone when I feel the need to voice my loud opinions. I've stood with other dads who yell even more than me. I've distracted myself with game day responsibilities like videotaping, working chain gang or concession stand, and even umping myself.

With husbands, some strategies work better than others. The ones that don't work include when a wife piles on guilt, loudly corrects her husband in public, points out all his flaws at once, turns the kids against him, threatens divorce, or withholds romantic favors.

Strategies that do work, I'd explain like this: For us, they're the direct result of Rita and my coming together and recommitting to the big picture. Our goal is to grow old together sharing mutual love and respect. Which means, her job is to never give up on me. A wife's best tools are prayer, love, tough love, wise counsel, patience, and perseverance.

So do yourself and your husband a favor. Have that one-on-one, heart-to-heart talk and get permission to lend him a hand as he works on his one fatal flaw.

Finally, when it comes to fixing an individual's biggest flaw—his or yours, for that matter—there's one more thing to remember. You can't do it on your own. Both of you are going to have to come together and ask God for help. He's got answers you won't find in this chapter or anywhere else.

Takeaway

It's difficult for any of us to admit when we're wrong. It's even more difficult to admit that we can't admit that we're wrong.

"Those who disregard discipline despise themselves, but the one who heeds correction gains understanding."

—Proverbs 15:32

A Husband Needs His Wife...

To Survive Your Mother-In-Law

Your husband loves his mom. She might drive him crazy. Or be creepily possessive. Or have all kinds of baggage. But she made him chicken soup when he was sniffly. She made sure his bath towels were fluffy. She cut the crusts off his peanut-butter-and-jelly samwiches. She was his first love.

You have every right to scream, "But he ain't married to her. He married me!" And you would be very accurate and blame-free. The day he slipped that ring on your finger, his sweet devoted mother took a demotion. She became the number-two woman in his life.

If a battle for your husband's heart or attention is not a problem, you may skip the rest of this chapter. But for some reason, that is not the case with many husbands.

Why do some newly married men cling so tightly to their mommy's apron strings? And why do mommies let them? I am not going to quote Freud or reference psychosexual oedipal issues. What I am going to say is, the Bible makes it very clear. Back in chapter 2, we looked at that passage from Genesis that is repeated in Matthew and Ephesians. Right after the creation of Adam and Eve, God himself defines the first priority of a marriage.

That is why a man leaves his father and mother and is united to his wife, and they become one flesh (Genesis 2:24).

The problem is that you might be *one flesh*, but you are not of *one mind*. He knows things you don't. His mom, for example. You don't know how she thinks. You don't know what's important to her. You don't even know the family traditions. In her enlightening book *The Mother-in-Law Dance*, Annie

Chapman shares the story of the terrifying and amusing first Christmas she spent with her new husband at his parents' house.

> It was quite a shock the first Christmas morning at my in-laws. Eventually, everyone got up and leisurely meandered into the living room. They sat around the Christmas tree, drinking coffee, talking, and munching on Christmas cookies. I kept waiting for the stampede toward the mountain of gifts located within arm's reach. But to my amazement, no one made a move toward the colorfully wrapped bounty under the Christmas tree. I asked what I considered to be a logical question: "When do we open the gifts?" They looked at me like I had crabs crawling out of my ears.
>
> My husband informed me in a rather hushed whisper, "We don't open gifts until after dinner." What? Who ever heard of going all Christmas Day without opening your gifts? At that moment I sincerely wondered, *What kind of nuthouse did I marry into?*[5]

The story illustrates the challenge of joining a new family with long-standing traditions and definite opinions. Your mother-in-law is the gatekeeper who is going to invite you to be part of the family or not. Thankfully you have a great weapon at your disposal—your husband. He should do everything possible to assure the two of you get along.

So here's the plan. Especially in the first months of marriage, but even years later, your husband needs to be an archaeologist and lighthouse. Before every interaction, he should be explaining critical family history and pointing out the jagged rocks you need to avoid. You need to know about Aunt Lu's inedible cornbread and Uncle Frank's not-so-secret toupee. You need to know that Sally isn't talking to Carly. And that cousin Mortimer thinks he's quite a ladies' man. You need to know old traditions and new relationships. As you dust and polish your own home to get ready for a visit from his parents or on the drive over to their place, insist he fill you in on what to expect. Don't let him brush you off by saying, "Oh, don't worry. Just be yourself." If he tells you not to worry and something goes terribly wrong, you have my (rare) permission to say, "I told you so!"

Annie Chapman urges you to appreciate, accept, and even look for ways to admire your mother-in-law. But she also insists that "the wife trumps mother every time."

The idea here, like so many uncomfortable marriage moments, is to see if you can avoid the conflagration *before* it flares up. If he doesn't get that, you need to remind him. While you're at it, do a quick mental checklist about your own family and their traditions, anomalies, and quirks. Then make sure your husband stays well informed.

Takeaway

Leave and cleave is more than a clever rhyme; it's a biblically sound mandate for marriage.

> *"The family you came from isn't as important*
> *as the family you're going to have."*
> —Ring Lardner (1885–1933)

A Husband Needs His Wife…

To Recommend Some Amusing Outings Once in a While

When we travel with kids or other couples—or just us—I am the one who grabs the tourist guides and AAA books or jumps online for interesting spots to visit or things to do.

Part of me wishes Rita would put a little more effort into proposing our sightseeing itinerary, but she knows I'm already going overboard. If we're at a sun-drenched resort, she's perfectly content to read a book on the beach. If we're in a big city, she would be perfectly happy strolling the sights within a few blocks of the hotel. If we're going to an obvious mecca of tourism, the top attractions are already clear. In Washington DC, it's the monuments. In Orlando, it's Walt Disney World. In Door County, the best plan is clearly just to walk the main-street shops and go to a fish boil.

Rita's philosophy is to let the destination reveal itself naturally. In other words, *a vacation should be a vacation.* Conversely, I think a vacation is a chance to do, do, and do things that you don't normally do. Our different approach to travel is more proof that successful marriages are built on overlapping and intertwining gifts and preferences.

For the sake of your marriage, may I suggest that you initiate, organize, or schedule an occasional just-for-fun excursion? Imagine the two of you on a romantic getaway to some well-known location for lovers. The Poconos, Paris, the Napa Valley, Bora-Bora, or that cute little town with all the bed-and-breakfasts two hours from your home.

But this chapter is not about romance. It's about trying something new together, doing something memorable, and reinvigorating your relationship. (Which I guess does end up helping in the romance department.)

Some ideas:

Segway tour. Quite a few cities and even some smaller towns offer a chance to jump on your very own two-wheeled, gyroscope-balanced vehicle and follow a tour guide through their bustling streets. You'll see sculptures, fountains, bridges, and other landmarks. But the funnest part is how remarkably easy Segways are to navigate.

Rent bikes, a tandem bike, canoes, kayaks, or Rollerblades. You'll burn some energy and will probably be without a tour guide. Which makes it all the more challenging and memorable for couples.

Canyon hiking, rock climbing, snorkeling, hang gliding, whitewater rafting, cross-country skiing, ziplining, or bungee jumping. Mostly for younger couples, but how old do you really feel?

Hot-air-balloon rides, horseback riding, Jeep tours, or renting a convertible for the weekend. Some adventures don't require you to be in peak physical shape. (If, like my bride, you happen to be allergic to horses...well let's not relive that horror.)

Frisbee golf. I can't recommend golf for couples. If you're both pretty good, then go for it. But for most couples, one laborious round of golf is a recipe for relational disaster. However, spending an hour or so at one of the many Frisbee-golf courses sprouting up around the country might be a delightful bonding experience as you learn the strategies and techniques together. You can call it exercise, but it's more like a walk in the park with a dose of competition.

Shooting range. There's something compelling and empowering about holding, aiming, and squeezing the trigger of a Colt, Ruger, or Smith & Wesson. Local firing ranges have all the rules and will keep you safe. Your husband will be blown away. Not literally.

Grab hard-to-get tickets. To a professional sporting event, rodeo, monster truck rally, symphony, or the reunion tour of your favorite rock band from high school.

Salsa dancing, ballroom dancing, or square dancing. I have no idea how your husband would react to such a suggestion. Maybe neither do you.

Horse-drawn carriage. Clip-clop through Central Park or around a small town square. Snuggle up and celebrate your life together.

Go back to high school. Even if you live far from your old hometown, head over to an occasional football game, choir concert, or theater production at your local high school.

Think like a tourist. If none of the above inspires you, then imagine you're visiting your zip code for one week only. What are the must-see sights and tours for an out-of-towner? Have you taken the tour of the local candy factory or been to the top floor of the tallest building in town? Walk your main drag and pretend you're seeing it for the first time.

A word of caution. Your husband will love that you're thinking of new ways to spend time with him. Unfortunately, your suggestion may catch him off guard, which may cause him to say something stupid...

"Where did that idea come from?" "We can't afford that right now." "What are the dates? I'm not sure about that weekend." "I did that before we were married and it's not fun at all."

Uggh. I confess these are the exact kind of words that come out of my mouth. When Rita does present a carefully thought-out idea for an amusing outing, I can't process the cost, the commitment, the calendar, and the health risks all at the same time. It might be because guys cannot multitask. Stupid me will almost always ask a question or raise a concern that just doesn't matter. Which is probably one of the reasons why she rarely makes excursion suggestions.

So be aware of that unfortunate possibility. Trust that after the idea settles into his brain, he will love it.

Other than that concern, go for it. It might be as easy as saying something like, "Wouldn't it be fun to rent a convertible for the weekend and drive up to Lake Geneva?"

Or just show the above list to your hubby and say, "Pick one."

Takeaway

When a husband and wife explore the world together, their greatest discovery is each other.

> *"The real voyage of discovery consists not in seeking*
> *new landscapes but in having new eyes."*
>
> —Marcel Proust (1871–1922)

A Husband Needs His Wife…

To Make Marriage Sexy Again

Just last week, Rita and I were skimming Netflix and we stumbled across the old Audrey Hepburn/Cary Grant movie titled *Charade*. Set in Paris, the 1963 film is filled with lighthearted suspense, comedic wordplay, and romantic teasing. It was great fun and I recommend it. It's got some dead bodies, but no blood. It's got two very attractive costars, but no sex. Not even implied sex where the camera pans away from the embracing couple and the music swells. The two weren't married, so the scriptwriters didn't include a sex scene.

The movie got me thinking about the media, our changing culture, and public displays of affection (PDA).

Today, if two characters in a movie express the slightest interest in each other, they jump in the sack. Later, they may (or may not) fall in love. But the Hollywood formula is to get that sex scene in the first reel to keep the audience interested. In other words, if *Charade* were made today, Audrey and Cary would have shown some skin early and often.

Not so with married couples in films. Hollywood makes it pretty clear that romance within marriage doesn't sell tickets. That's not interesting. That's not provocative.

Women's magazines have also done a disservice to marriage. At one time, cover stories and articles in popular magazines like *Cosmopolitan* and *Redbook* would feature articles like "Your Husband's Biggest Secret" or "How to Drive Your Hubby Wild." Sometime in the 1980s, the editors of women's magazines stopped using the word "husband." Now they use the term "your boyfriend," "your guy," or "your man." It's as if husbands (and marriage for that matter) are no longer relevant.

Nowadays on television, very few married couples even hint at a satisfying sex life. Going back several years, Cliff and Claire Huxtable would share a suggestive phrase or two on *The Cosby Show*. I guess Homer Simpson sometimes switches off the light in their bedroom and we hear Marge coo, "Oh Homie," but that's a cartoon, for goodness' sake. But if you're a single TV character living in Manhattan or Southern California, anything goes.

One more example of the culture getting it backward. Why is it that married women are embarrassed to go into Victoria's Secret, but teenage girls aren't?

At this point, I could begin a multipage rant about our decaying social values. I could trace the crumbling of morality to the 1963 Supreme Court decision to ban state-sponsored prayer in public schools. I could blame Elvis Presley, the birth-control pill, Hugh Hefner, Betsy Friedan, *Roe v. Wade*, Watergate, Woodstock, disco, or something in the drinking water. But that rant would probably not be fair and probably not help do anything to elevate the sanctity and satisfaction of any marriage.

Since we can't count on Hollywood, the media, or retailers, let's take it upon ourselves to reclaim romance for husbands and wives everywhere and hold it up for the world to see. Here's my plan for making marriage sexy again.

What if all the committed married couples we know began to hold hands when taking a walk around neighborhood? Or kissed each other hello and goodbye—even in public? What would our kids think if they saw Mom and Dad giving each other a nice long smooch right in the kitchen? The goal would be to make your third-grader say, "Ewww" or your teenager say, "Get a room."

Finally, how about if once or twice a year all married couples made a vow to get away to a bed-and-breakfast or nice hotel just for a night or weekend. And even tell family and friends where you're going! The purpose is obvious. There's nothing to be ashamed of.

Don't you think that would improve the image of marriage for all involved? Besides, it's a good excuse for an extra smooch or cuddle. So what do you say?

We could call it "The PDA in Marriage Project." Go to my website—jaypayleitner.com—find my e-mail address, and let me know if you're in. Or if I'm way off base.

Takeaway

A recent study revealed that the most satisfying sex happens in long-term marriage relationships. That's more good news that should be eagerly shared.

> *"And he took her in his arms and kissed her under the sunlit sky, and he cared not that they stood high upon the walls in the sight of many."*
> —J.R.R. TOLKIEN (1892–1973)

A Husband Needs His Wife...

To Be Last at the Cross and First at the Tomb

In the Bible, it seems many of the male characters are often out fishing, boasting on street corners, hiding in caves and upper rooms, thinking lecherous thoughts on rooftops, arguing among themselves, throwing rocks, and starting wars.

On the other hand, many of the women in the Bible are making choices that matter. The woman at the well is listening to Jesus and conveying his words of truth back to her community. The poor widow is dropping her last two copper mites in the collection box. One young woman even responded, "May it happen to me as you have said,"[6] when an angel told her she would give birth to the Son of God.

And let us not forget Mary Magdalene. Despite some misrepresentations in church history and even recent movies, she was a true disciple and perhaps as close to Jesus as any of the 12 apostles. The Gospel of Luke explains how Jesus cast out seven demons from Mary of Magdala and places her as one of the few women traveling from town to town with Jesus and the apostles. Her caring heart led her to stand beside Jesus' mother at the crucifixion. Three days later, she went to Jesus' tomb at sunrise to anoint the body with spices. That morning, she was the first to see the stone rolled away, chatted with an angel, and was the first to see the risen Christ. The Gospel of Matthew records that she, after seeing the empty tomb, was "afraid yet filled with joy, and ran to tell his disciples" (Matthew 28:8). And by the way, those thick-headed disciples didn't believe her story.

Inspiration can come from any character in the Bible, man or woman.

But you have to appreciate how Mary Magdalene stood by the Savior in his darkest hour while most of the disciples were hiding in fear that the authorities were coming for them next.

By all accounts, she was independent, courageous, bold, and persevering. She wasn't a prostitute, a rumor which may have begun with Pope Gregory in the sixth century and was made popular on Broadway in *Jesus Christ Superstar* and in movies such as *The Last Temptation of Christ* and Mel Gibson's *The Passion of the Christ*. Biblical scholars confirm that she was not the sister of Martha, the woman who anointed Jesus' feet with oil, or the woman who was saved from stoning. Mary Magdalene was saved by Christ and, in return, gave her life back to him.

That's a pretty good formula for any life. If you have not previously thought of Mary Magdalene as a hero, then maybe you ought to reconsider. For many modern believers, her story is simply misunderstood. But she was a survivor with a past, a follower with a servant's heart, and a partner in grief to Jesus' mother. As an eyewitness to the evidence for the resurrection she became the first bold witness sharing the greatest news of all time.

Can you imagine a better role model for women who claim to follow Christ? You can't slap a one- or two-word label on Mary Magdalene.

And that shouldn't be the case with you either. How would you describe yourself? Wife, mom, homemaker, sales representative, accountant, doctor, lawyer, nurse, teacher, bus driver, diaper changer, homework supervisor, bedtime reader, school volunteer, alderman, governor, secretary, CEO, author, coach, electrical engineer, florist, stamp collector, expert marksman, lieutenant, seamstress, cookie baker, artist, sister, daughter, friend, butcher, baker, or candlestick maker?

I hope you chose more than one role from that list. And I hope you came up with a few other descriptors not on the list. I also hope some of those titles were chosen by you in conversation with God. But I also believe it's okay to allow your marriage partner to request you to take on some responsibilities you wouldn't necessarily choose for yourself. That's how it's supposed to work in a godly marriage. If he has shortcomings, she might need to step up and fill in the gaps. And vice versa.

Put another way, being a woman with multiple gifts and multiple responsibilities is so much more fulfilling than simply boxing yourself into one role.

Coming full circle, let me encourage you to cherish your own relationship with Jesus. Listen to him like the woman at the well. Sacrifice of yourself like the poor widow. And like Mary Magdalene, don't be afraid to sit at the foot of the cross and consider the magnitude of what happened there. Then, recognize the significance of the empty tomb and boldly tell others that Jesus still lives.

Takeaway

Men have been assigned the role of spiritual leaders of the home, but every woman must bring her own talents and her own passions to partner in family leadership.

> *"Each of you should use whatever gift you have received to serve others, as faithful stewards of God's grace in its various forms. If anyone speaks, they should do so as one who speaks the very words of God. If anyone serves, they should do so with the strength God provides, so that in all things God may be praised through Jesus Christ."*
> —1 PETER 4:10-11

A Husband Needs His Wife…

To Make the Bed (or Not)

Half this book was written after midnight. That's my most productive time of day. No phone calls. No Twitter alerts. No hunger pangs. No wondering if the mail lady has come yet. No sunlight beckoning me outside for a walk or a dog run. When I'm on book deadline, several nights a week after the late local news, Rita will find me in my office and kiss me goodnight. Upstairs in bed, she'll drift off while reading her Nook. Downstairs, I'm clacking away on my MacBook Pro. (I'm hoping those subtle product placements will get me some free stuff or maybe an endorsement deal.)

For some reason late night is prime time for my axon terminals to fire off their most productive neurotransmissions across my synaptic gaps. I'll zero in on an idea that's been kicking around my head, and a solid first draft of a chapter magically flows through my fingers.

All of which means I get to bed late. Which means I get up an hour after Rita. Which means I make the bed. Because that's our deal. Whoever gets up last makes the bed. I'm not sure who came up with it. But that's our deal.

I confess, she makes a better bed than I do. A good percentage of the time, I fail in my efforts to arrange the dozen decorative pillows to her exact specifications. Quite often, the purposeless pillows don't even make it back on the bed. Still, I hold up my end of the bargain and I am chief bedmaker almost every day. Sometimes as an ever-so-thoughtful gift to my bride, I'll stack the dozen odd-shaped decorative pillows in an artistic geometric sculpture at the foot of the bed. She rarely appreciates my art.

What other similar deals do we have? First person up gets the newspapers from the driveway and makes the coffee. (Which usually means Rita, of course.) Whoever is not busy at the moment picks up the middle-school athlete after practice. When company is coming, Jay vacuums. Otherwise, it's Rita's job. We wash windows, trim hedges, and rake leaves together.

For many household tasks, our deal includes a more clearly defined division of duties. Snow-shoveling, answering the phone, cleaning up puke, picking up dog poop, taking out the trash, doing taxes, mowing the lawn, and annually painting the porch are my territory.

Tasks which have always been on Rita's plate include paying bills, laundry, filling the dishwasher, weekday dinners, school stuff, insurance and doctor stuff, remembering birthdays, feeding the dog, and rearranging the furniture every two months.

I'm sure you and your husband have similar deals. Some tasks are shared; some are clearly assigned to one or the other. Often it comes down to passions, giftedness, time, and some unspoken factors. For instance, when Rita attempts to clean up puke, there's a high likelihood of more puking. Rita can tolerate the sound of an unanswered phone—I cannot. A few dishes in the sink have never bothered me—not so for my bride. I like shoveling snow. Rita knows all that confusing medical jargon. If I were in charge of feeding the dog, we might not have one anymore.

So what's the point? I guess this chapter is a salute to the partnership of marriage. Everything has to get done. And somehow it does. Much of the productivity plan for the Payleitner home evolved without a lot of communication. It just happened. And there's actually very little complaining. Sometimes I hate mowing the lawn, sometimes it's a delightful break in the day. Does Rita like e-mailing and talking to insurance companies? Heavens no. But she's a master at maneuvering through the maze of claims adjusters and their managers.

I hope your household runs like a well-oiled machine. If not, you might try reassigning some of your daily, weekly, and annual tasks. The division of duties doesn't have to be set in stone. Since Rita's election to city council, I've been doing a little more meal prep. Two decades ago I tried my hand at paying the bills, but I made some miscalculations that we're still paying for. Rita reminds me that she mowed the lawn for about a decade—even though we had four growing boys at the time. Go figure. I even loaded the dishwasher once. Rita had to rearrange several plates, glasses, and utensils because I "did it wrong." Some days the bed doesn't get made.

One change came as surprise to me. For the first 15 years, Rita and I made it a point to go to bed at the same time. I never imagined there would come a time when that routine changed. But such is the rhythm of married life. So here I sit typing these words with Rita a staircase away. And it's okay.

It's tremendously important to respect and hold tightly to family traditions. But as kids get older and circumstances change, sometimes we need to let traditions live in our memories while we make room for new ones.

Just so with marriage deals. As long as they work, let them work in your favor. But if you or your husband wants to swap roles or tweak the schedule, go for it. Just make sure there's a mutual appreciation for what each of you do for the sake of the family.

As for me, I'm going to bed.

Takeaway

I don't know how single parents get it all done. Maybe they don't.

"A loud and cheerful greeting early in the morning will be taken as a curse!"

—Proverbs 27:14 NLT

A Husband Needs His Wife…

To Follow Her Heart When It Comes to Careers and Kids

Because I'm a guy, I cannot say something as chauvinistic as "real women want to be homemakers." That would cause many female readers to gently close this book and slip it in the recycling bin.

Instead, I'll do what journalists do—point to the latest study. A 2011 study by NBC Universal explains that at this time in history only 4 percent of families fall under the U.S. Census definition of "traditional"—that is, "a working father and a stay-at-home mother with kids under 18." How does that minuscule number strike you? Does it sound healthy for America? Let's dig a little deeper.

The goal of the study was to identify the best strategies for advertisers to speak to today's moms. It seems the surge of fragmented families and uncertain economic conditions have created a backlash of women seeking more traditional values. Melissa Lavigne-Delville, VP of Trends and Strategic Insights at NBCU, said, "Although moms are not saying they want to go back to the 1950s, they are clinging to certain values and traditions associated with that time period."[7]

Two of the more interesting stats jumped off the page:[8]

- 66 percent of moms say they would rather be a stay-at-home parent than a working parent;
- 53 percent of employed moms feel that while financially they need to work, they would prefer to be stay-at-home moms.

What these moms are saying is that they have a God-given desire to "do the mom thing." If you've given birth or adopted a baby, you very likely have experienced that yourself. Even if a woman loves her career, almost every new mommy has a very hard time severing her maternal ties in order to go back to work for six to ten hours every day. Sometimes the depth of feeling and maternal connection surprises them. Waiting for the baby, they fully expected to take a three-month leave of absence and then jump right back into the old routine. But after holding their baby they just couldn't do it.

If you have that feeling, don't brush it away. It's healthy. It's appropriate. Maybe there are options you haven't even considered. For a season of life, maybe you and your family can survive on one or one-and-a-half salaries. Maybe that season lasts until the kids go to elementary school, to middle school, to high school, or off to college.

No matter what—even if you earn half the family income or more—you need to share those kinds of feelings with your husband. After taking in all the facts and figures, he might say, "Our budget couldn't take the hit." Or he might say, "I was hoping you'd say that. We're going to make it work."

Sacrifices might need to be made. Cheaper vacations. More modest Christmases. Less caviar, more mac and cheese. A few more years out of the old clunker. What it might come down to is this: More important than a *big home* is for mom to *be home*.

Does that sound old-fashioned? It's not. According to the research, it's not common, but it's what two-thirds of women want. And it may be very practical.

I am not going to do all the math. But I dare you to add up the cost of day care, transportation, business clothing, dry cleaning, lunches, fast-food dinners, and extra formula. That relatively simple exercise will help you realize that your take-home pay isn't all making it home. Then add the expense of a few extra doctor visits because of the latest viruses fermenting at that daycare center. Then consider how your income (which is mostly outgo) puts you in a higher tax bracket.

I speak from experience. Thirty years ago, Rita had been recruited by a local real-estate agent to get into the business. I was encouraging because we certainly needed the money and I thought it was something she wanted. As she was about to drop Alec off at a day-care provider for the first time ever, she realized she couldn't do it. I'll quote my wife directly: "No one can take better care of my baby than me. How could they? No one loves that baby more than me."

Of course, every situation is different. You need to talk, pray, get wise counsel, and do what's best for your family. Maybe Mom can work part-time from home. Maybe Grandma or Aunt Sue would be thrilled to love on your little one a few times per week. Maybe Dad stays home. That trend was also well-noted in the NBCU study.

It's a cliché, but the time will go by very quickly. Spending 5 to 18 years as a *mostly mom* may temporarily knock you off a career path, but the rewards are greater than you can imagine.

The point is, you should not dismiss your maternal instinct. If you're supposed to stay home, do whatever it takes. The follow-up point is just as critical. Please do not feel guilty if you find great satisfaction in a career that has meaning and merit. I have no doubt that you will make sure your offspring are well taken care of.

To summarize. Between you and your husband, figure out the best way for you to be the mom God is calling you to be. For my five kids, somehow Rita was able to stay home. And it worked. Money was tight, but we made it. What's more, I'm happy to report that Rita's sense of purpose and value didn't suffer. It flourished.

During the years she was "only a housewife," she did amazing things impacting thousands of lives for the better. She grew from classroom and church volunteer to PTO president for two different schools. Then to president of the high-school athletic booster club. Now she's an alderman for the City of St. Charles. (Which reduces me to mere arm candy, and I couldn't be more proud.)

Still, her favorite title, and one she wears well, is "stay-at-home mom for almost 30 years."

Takeaway

The kids may never be able to put into words the sacrifices you make for them, but they will know you did.

"If you bungle raising your children, I don't think
whatever else you do well matters very much."
—JACQUELINE KENNEDY ONASSIS (1929–1994)

A Husband Needs His Wife…

To Realize You Can't Nag Him into the Kingdom

Like everyone, your husband has to make his own decision for Christ. Also, he has to choose for himself to lead his family spiritually.

In addition, here's another truth you likely know but has not been grasped by a handful of other readers. You can't nag your husband to go to church or to begin a relationship with Jesus.

I'm not being flippant. This is a huge concern for women in every church in the country. This Sunday, 13 million more women than men will attend church. But sometimes you can't blame the guys. Church has a lot of competition for your husband on Sundays: golf, football, sleeping late, a nice thick Sunday newspaper, a day off after a busy six-day workweek, your honey-do list, and his own established belief system or lack thereof.

Perhaps the biggest reason guys aren't drawn to church might be because it feels like surrender. Often the church experience is kind of wimpy. The music is sentimental. The people are all a little too nice. The theme of most Sunday sermons is, "Do nice things and don't do bad things."

Guys don't want to be told to be nice. They want to hang out in a place where they can flex their muscles, spit, adjust their jockstraps, and rescue an occasional damsel in distress. Especially on weekends! Many guys spend all week saying "Yes" to their bosses and customers. On the weekend, they want to do something significant, not sit in a pew with their hands folded.

Of course, the authentic Christian life is a bold, courageous battle worth fighting. The church needs warriors. But most guys never see that side of following Jesus.

If you're the wife of a man who isn't engaged in, seeking, or excited about spiritual truth, you need a plan. Right now your marriage relationship is disconnected. You and your husband's goals and standards are different. You're probably in constant conflict about all kinds of things, including how to spend your money, raising kids, where to vacation, movies, friends, recreation, and the core values of right and wrong. You're serving two different masters. That's one reason the Bible teaches, "Do not be yoked together with unbelievers" (2 Corinthians 6:14).

But if you find yourself in such a relationship, think of it this way. As a couple, you're halfway there. So, besides nagging, how can you get your husband to open his heart and mind to spiritual truth?

First and foremost, don't give up on him:

> For those who are married, I have a command that comes not from me, but from the Lord. A wife must not leave her husband. But if she does leave him, let her remain single or else be reconciled to him (1 Corinthians 7:10 NLT).

Stay committed to him. Then, let your example—not your words—draw him to seek a new, better way to live:

> In the same way, you wives must accept the authority of your husbands. Then, even if some refuse to obey the Good News, your godly lives will speak to them without any words. They will be won over by observing your pure and reverent lives (1 Peter 3:1-2 NLT).

Along the way, let him know that Christianity isn't for wimps. Tell him about some of the spiritual battles you're facing. He may want to come to your rescue and even begin to realize he doesn't own the right battle gear:

> Be strong in the Lord and in his mighty power. Put on the full armor of God, so that you can take your stand against the devil's schemes. For our struggle is not against flesh and blood, but against the rulers, against the authorities, against the powers of this dark world and against the spiritual forces of evil in the heavenly realms (Ephesians 6:10-12).

As you join him in the battle for his life, don't stop praying for him. And pray expectantly. Look for signs of spiritual growth:

> We continually ask God to fill you with the knowledge of his will through all the wisdom and understanding that the Spirit gives, so that you may live a life worthy of the Lord and please him in every way: bearing fruit in every good work, growing in the knowledge of God (Colossians 1:9-10).

Serve your husband:

> Serve wholeheartedly, as if you were serving the Lord, not people, because you know that the Lord will reward each one for whatever good they do (Ephesians 6:7-8).

Don't count on your own words, but count on the Holy Spirit:

> My message and my preaching were not with wise and persuasive words, but with a demonstration of the Spirit's power (1 Corinthians 2:4).

During rough patches, exhibit joy:

> Now is your time of grief, but I will see you again and you will rejoice, and no one will take away your joy (John 16:22).

Then be ready. One day your husband's eyes will open and he will realize that he's heading the wrong direction and needs to find a new path. He's going to see you in a new light. And he may even realize he has a God-shaped hole in his heart. That's when you gently and respectfully tell him you love him, tell him you're committed to him, but then tell him the real source of your deepest joy:

> Always be prepared to give an answer to everyone who asks you to give the reason for the hope that you have. But do this with gentleness and respect (1 Peter 3:15).

And then just smile, be humble, and stay open to God's leading, because right about that time, He will provide the perfect opening. An event, a person, a cause, maybe even a tragedy, that will help your husband recognize his need for a Savior.

I know you want to be there when he finally makes a decision to follow Christ. That would be sweet. But no matter when it happens, first rejoice, then be grateful, and then be ready to see a man truly on fire for God. Your husband. Who would have thought!

Takeaway

If you really love him, then love him into God's family.

"There has got abroad a notion, somehow, that if you become a Christian you must sink your manliness and turn milksop."

—Charles Spurgeon (1834–1892)

A Husband Needs His Wife...

To Learn the Lessons of the Nap

For years, I didn't understand the concept of taking a nap. Comic-strip characters like Dagwood, Beetle Bailey, and Hagar the Horrible were always curling up on a sofa or anyplace they could grab a nap undisturbed. When the kids were small, Rita bought me a hammock for Father's Day, and I don't think I fell asleep in it even once.

Well I'm over 50 now. Not old. But definitely appreciative of catching a few z's in the middle of the afternoon. Especially if I had a productive morning. One day earlier this month, my brain was getting foggy, which is usually a signal that it's time for a quick snooze. Rita was the only other person in the house, and here are the words that came out of my mouth. "I think I'm going to lie down for a twenty-minute nap...unless you have a better idea."

Before you say, "Oh no, this chapter is about how men need a quickie once in a while," let me continue. For the record, Rita did not take me up on option number two. An afternoon of intimacy would have been a nice distraction and probably would have re-energized me better than any nap. And frankly, I do recommend you take full advantage of that marital option when the time is right, but that's just a side note and bonus lesson for this chapter.

What Rita did do was join me for a nap. An honest-to-goodness, middle-of-the-day, keep-your-clothes-on nap. As I do for most naps, I flopped across the comforter on our king-size bed, perpendicular to my nighttime sleeping angle. Rita lay close enough so that I could feel her presence and warmth and hear the rhythm of her breathing as it became in synch with mine. It was nice.

Jealous? Sure you are. Naps are one of those gifts that many people don't fully appreciate. But when the stresses and deadlines of the world pile up, a nap is a much better answer than alcohol, drugs, energy drinks, or yelling at your co-workers or family. A slew of medical studies reveal that napping improves memory, reduces on-the-job accidents, and boosts memory and creativity. One study on sleepy astronauts at NASA found a 40-minute nap improved performance by 34 percent and alertness by 100 percent.[9]

Dear reader, if you're a young mother with kids nipping at your ankles, you're surely saying, "You've got to be kidding, Jay. My next nap is probably 15 years away." If you spend your days running from one meeting to another, the idea of mid-afternoon naps may seem even further away. Your favorite verse from all of Scripture might be Psalm 55:6: "Oh, that I had the wings of a dove! I would fly away and be at rest."

Well then, it's time to reveal the actual lesson of this chapter. The question is not whether you should be taking more naps or doing more of anything. The real question is, "Should you be doing less?"

The myth of the superwoman doing it all is indeed a myth. You know your schedule, and I wouldn't dare try to list all the stuff you need to accomplish each and every week. But friend, if you're constantly on the edge of overload, you need to intentionally remove some of that burden. And you're the only one who can do it. Learn to say things that reduce your load at work, at church, at your kid's school, and at home:

"I'd love to, but I won't be able to help out this time."

"Let me give you Carla's phone number."

"For dinner tonight, do you want to order a pizza or Chinese takeout?"

"Oh wonderful husband, I'm letting you watch the kids for the evening. And I'm taking a nice long bath."

The truth is that husbands like our wives stress-free and relaxed. It makes our own lives so much easier. If we can help you arrange a guilt-free bath, nap, or evening off, that makes us feel like we're succeeding on the home front. We don't say it out loud, but we are well aware that women take on more responsibilities at home and in the community. We actually would like you to slow down just a bit. So keep doing all the stuff that you enjoy and has meaning and purpose. But for our sake, see if you can trim some of the stuff that causes you the most frustration and doesn't make a difference in the long run.

And for heaven's sake, take a nap once in a while. Which, of course, means that your husband can take one too. Unless you have a better idea.

Takeaway

Wives and mothers who go 90 miles an hour all day every day will eventually crash. It's better if you decide when and where that is, rather than waiting for it to happen at the worst possible time.

> *"Come to me, all you who are weary and*
> *burdened, and I will give you rest."*
>
> —MATTHEW 11:28

A Husband Needs His Wife...

To Keep Him in the Loop

Recently, I went through a long period of time when I thought I must be the most self-absorbed person on the planet. I kept finding myself in conversations in which I felt like a total outsider.

Every week or so, we would run into some old friends and Rita would already know everything going on in their lives. One daughter is studying in Paris, another daughter is a sophomore at Calvin College, and their son and daughter-in-law just delivered twins. How did Rita know? And what was wrong with me? I care about people. Sure, Rita gets out of the house more than I do, but I'm not a hermit. Where was she getting this data, and how was she staying so current with people we rarely ever see?

Well, you already know where this is going.

A recent survey by Harris Interactive commissioned by Rebtel looked at the U.S. online adult population. They discovered that 68 percent of women use social networks and media to stay in touch with friends, compared to 54 percent of men. The pollsters even did the math, which revealed that 22 million more women than men communicate with friends via Facebook and so on.

Facebook! That's why I—along with a bunch of other husbands—feel out of the loop. And I can't help but wonder if the same thing is happening in your home.

So now here's where this chapter gets tricky. Husbands really do want the scoop on some things but not so much on other things. For example, if the neighbor's poodle gets swooped off by a hawk, that's a tasty news tidbit. If your aunt's guppy dies, you can keep that to yourself. We certainly want to know if a young person is going to attend our alma mater or the same school as one of our children, but we won't remember the name of any other college. When dear friends have a new kid or grandkid, we want to share the joy. But unless it's an extraordinary number, please don't bother us with the newborn's height, weight, or Apgar score. If you hear that the second baseman on our softball team rips his ACL, please let us know. But if our second cousin's plumber's girlfriend has tendinitis, we are not going to put that on our prayer list.

True confession: Actually, we are part hermit. Guys are probably a little more self-absorbed than gals. We sort of do live in our own little world and care more about stuff that impacts our lives directly. That's why our eyes glaze over when you tell us the color of the bridesmaids' dresses at a wedding we weren't even invited to. That's why we stop watching four seconds into the YouTube video of Irish step-dancing by your college roommate's daughter. That's why we count on you...to filter out the frivolous and make sure we don't miss that which is noteworthy and compelling.

And oh my goodness, 97 percent of the stuff on Pinterest puts us into an instant stupor from which only three sounds can snap us out: a referee's whistle, monster truck engine, or a microwave timer. A good wife would know that.

Takeaway

In the car, on the way to key social events, please give your husband three facts—but no more than that—that he needs to know about the host or other key guests. Include things to notice and mention. Or more important, things to not notice and not mention. His reputation is in your hands.

"Privacy is dead, and social media holds the smoking gun."
—Pete Cashmore

A Husband Needs His Wife...

To Hit Bottom with Him

As you may recall, chapter 5 chronicles my eclectic work history and how Rita stuck with me through some unpleasant and abrupt job changes. How our marriage survived one of those tumultuous seasons makes a nice story. Here it is:

Once upon a time a boy named Jay was full of optimism and potential. Plus he was kinda cute, so Rita said yes when Jay got on one knee and presented her with a huge one-quarter-carat diamond ring. The fact that he had not achieved much didn't matter, because his new wife had a great deal of faith in her young husband.

Until she didn't.

You see, before long Jay and Rita had two small boys and were a couple months behind in their FHA mortgage. Silly Jay was trying to earn a living selling law books to corporate attorneys and he was not very good at it. He slogged around the Chicago Loop carrying a 26-pound briefcase filled with samples. His three polyester three-piece suits were getting shabbier and shabbier. His lone pair of black wingtips that had once belonged to his grandfather had holes in their soles. Every month, he got further and further behind in his sales quotas.

Still, even in the midst of his job angst, Jay and Rita's life was not all bad. Their two boys were healthy and smart. They were plugged in to a good church and even had friends praying for them. Every evening, Rita kissed her husband and asked about his day. That was a good thing. And sometimes a hard thing.

For guys, their identity and self-esteem is often wrapped up in the success they experience on the job. Maybe it shouldn't be, but it is. Jay's optimism was disappearing. His potential seemed nowhere to be found. The world Jay had once hoped to conquer was beating him up and dragging him down. Rita still loved him. Which is why she did what she did.

She could have screamed at Jay to work harder. She could have pretended everything was okay. She could have taken the two boys and moved home to her mom and dad's house. She could have complained to all her friends and made his life miserable until he moved out.

Instead, she spoke. Rita did not raise her voice. She did not accuse. As she sat on the floor of their tiny living room, she looked at her husband standing in the kitchen doorway and said, "I don't have faith in you anymore."

It hurt Jay to hear that. But somehow, it was the exact right words at the exact right time. Rita was telling Jay that he was not alone. They were partners and any crisis needed to be faced with honesty, commitment, and communication. As he stood in the doorway, Jay experienced the worst and best moment of his life.

No, he didn't become a better salesman. That would have been impossible. But Jay did write those seven words on a 3x5 card and pushpin it on the wall above his desk: *"I don't have faith in you anymore."* Jay stopped feeling sorry for himself. He hustled a little more. He reevaluated his gifts, passions, and career options. Jay and Rita intentionally spent more time talking about goals, hopes, dreams, and God's plan for their lives.

That summer, Jay changed careers. His first job as an entry-level copywriter position at a small advertising agency on Michigan Avenue was a direct result of those husband-and-wife talks about all the things that really matter. When Jay told Rita the new job would actually reduce their income, she didn't hesitate. The young mother proved once again that she knew her husband and knew exactly what he needed to hear. Rita said, "We'll make it work."

A quarter century later, Jay still can't sell anything. But the bills are getting paid, their four sons have college degrees, their daughter is at West Point, and no one has missed a meal. And Rita and Jay have one more little joke that gets sprinkled into their current conversations about goals, hopes, dreams, and God's plan for their lives. Jay will say, "Do you have faith in me?" And Rita gets a twinkle in her eye and says, "For now."

And they lived happily ever after.

Takeaway

When you hit bottom—and I hope you do—make sure you and your husband fall together down into the darkness of the abyss. It will take both of you reaching, lifting, boosting, and supporting each other to crawl out into the sun. There's a very good chance that it's God who allowed you to fall. But don't be angry with him, because he is also the One who pulls you out to set your feet on solid rock.

> *"You may not realize it when it happens, but a kick in the teeth may be the best thing in the world for you."*
>
> —WALT DISNEY (1901–1966)

A Husband Needs His Wife...

To Fight Fair

M en can't get hysterical. Literally, they cannot. The word comes from the Greek word *hystera*, which, of course, means "womb." Which means only women suffer from *hysteria*, a word that Webster defines as "a psychoneurosis marked by emotional excitability and disturbances of the psychic, sensory, vasomotor, and visceral functions."

On behalf of all men everywhere, may I request that, since we don't have that same weapon in our arsenal, you refrain from being hysterical during any wife-husband confrontation? Now that we have that out of the way, let's move on to a much more dangerous tactic often used by the female of the species. That is when you get "historical."

Full disclosure and not a surprise: Men make mistakes. We forget anniversaries. We say thoughtless things about your mother, your girlfriends, your cooking, and your new haircut. We display our anger in inappropriate ways. We leave socks on the floor and toilet seats up. We say we were listening when we weren't. We promise to pick up milk, but we forget. We look too long at the curvy jogger. We spit, scratch, belch, and chew with our mouth open.

The list continues, but I'll stop now before I dig too deep of a hole. I also hope you fully realize that other lists could be assembled that itemize male positive attributes as well as potential female shortcomings. Every individual is different, but we must admit there are male tendencies and there are female tendencies.

And one of your tendencies may be to remind us husbands of our past sins even when they have nothing to do with today's crimes.

For example, let's say one Saturday afternoon we're making ourselves a PB&J and out the kitchen window we see the dog in the backyard digging up your flowerbed. With our sandwich in hand, we race outside to collar the canine, and we even feel a little heroic for rescuing your precious petunias. Twenty minutes later, you track us down in the garage and go off for several minutes because we left a mess on the kitchen counter. Okay, fine, maybe we deserve it. But then you cross the line. Your hysterical rant ends up getting historical when you say, "Every time you make a sandwich you expect me to clean up after you. Is your bowling team coming over to make tacos again?"

Whoa. The bowling-team taco incident was four years ago. What's more, in recent months we actually have been doing much better at cleaning up after ourselves in the kitchen. Plus, we were distracted by the digging dog.

Now don't you feel bad for getting all historical?

Bringing up past indiscretions and old issues is something we all do. But it's a good reminder that when wives and husbands have disagreements (loud or not-so-loud) to stick to the main points of the dispute. Don't drag old girlfriends or other irritations into the quarrel. If the topic is the electric bill and how too many lights are left on in the house, it doesn't help when you bring up the cost of new bowling shoes or your husband reminds you how much you paid for that Coach purse.

So here are the ground rules for fighting fair during your next argument. If you like, you may want to share these rules with your husband:

1. Stay on topic.

2. Don't raise your voice.

3. Try to see your spouse's perspective.

4. Determine if there may be an underlying misunderstanding or miscommunication. (Maybe you're both really after the same thing—clean counters, obedient pets, happy bowlers, pretty flower gardens.)

5. If there truly is a difference of opinion, see if you can come to some kind of compromise.

One of the great ways to stop a squabble in its tracks is to insert God into the equation and take yourself out. It's a real-world application of John 3:30, "He must increase, but I must decrease" (NASB).

Learning to fight fair is one of those marriage skills that didn't show up in your premarital counseling or marriage vows. The art of fighting fair only comes from a couple who are committed to looking out for what's best for each other. That's you and your devoted husband, right?

Takeaway

A spousal attack filled with half-truths and unconfirmed accusations will drive a wedge between a husband and wife. But if approached with respect, a nice heated argument can actually bring you closer together. If you let it.

"Marriage is the only war in which you sleep with the enemy."
—Francois de La Rochefoucauld (1613–1680)

A Husband Needs His Wife...

To Laugh at Marriage

I love quotations. Writing and researching this book and its counterpoint, *52 Things Wives Need from Their Husbands*, I perused hundreds of quotations on marriage. About two-thirds were unusable because they had a regretful, negative view of marriage. I had promised myself—and my publisher and readers—that I would not paint marriage as a terrible burden that we are forced to survive with gritted teeth and a broken spirit.

However, I found myself chuckling at quite a few of those "negative" quotes on marriage. Many of them even had a point. Because—as you know—many a truth is said in jest. So in my book for husbands, I included a chapter of about 20 quotations that present a cynical, jaundiced view of marriage.

Since then I have collected another 20, and here they are. For your husband's sake, I hope you have a good laugh. But not too good.

Marriage is a fine institution, but I'm not ready for an institution.
—MAE WEST

By all means marry; if you get a good wife, you'll become happy; if you get a bad one, you'll become a philosopher.
—SOCRATES

The only reason my wife agreed to marry me is because Christian Bale wasn't around to propose to her.
—JAROD KINTZ

*There is one thing more exasperating than a wife who can
cook and won't, and that's a wife who can't cook and will.*

—Robert Frost

My wife and I were happy for twenty years. Then we met.

—Rodney Dangerfield

*"I am" is reportedly the shortest sentence in the English
language. Could it be that "I do" is the longest sentence?*

—George Carlin

*The only time a woman really succeeds in
changing a man is when he's a baby.*

—Natalie Wood

To catch a husband is an art; to hold him is a job.

—Simone de Beauvoir

*Marriage is the alliance of two people, one of whom never
remembers birthdays and the other of whom never forgets them.*

—Ogden Nash

*I never married because there was no need. I have three pets
at home which answer the same purpose as a husband. I have
a dog which growls every morning, a parrot which swears
all afternoon, and a cat that comes home late at night.*

—Marie Corelli

*My wife tells me she doesn't care what I do when
I'm away, as long as I'm not enjoying it.*

—Lee Trevino

*Marriage is nature's way of ensuring that a woman picks up
some mothering experience before she has her first child.*

—Robert Brault

We always hold hands. If I let go, she shops.

—Henny Youngman

Men who have a pierced ear are better prepared for
marriage—they've experienced pain and bought jewelry.
—RITA RUDNER

A successful man is one who makes more money than his wife can
spend. A successful woman is one who can find such a man.
—LANA TURNER

If the grass looks greener on the other side of the
fence, it's because they take better care of it.
—CECIL SELIG

The Wedding March always reminds me of the
music played when soldiers go into battle.
—HEINRICH HEINE

Many a man in love with a dimple makes the
mistake of marrying the whole girl.
—STEPHEN LEACOCK

When women are depressed, they eat or go
shopping. Men invade another country.
—ELAYNE BOOSLER

Why get married and make one man miserable when I
can stay single and make thousands miserable?
—CARRIE P. SNOW

Did you immediately recognize your husband in any of the above one-liners? I hope not. I hope you fall asleep every night and get up every morning truly believing you are the luckiest girl in the world and thanking God for the institution of marriage that unites you with the most wonderful boy in the world.

Since that's not possible, let me say this. I'm a longtime believer in the idea of self-fulfilling prophecy. If you expect a crummy ball-and-chain marriage, you increase the chances that you'll experience exactly that.

Besides, comedians, playwrights, and essayists make their living saying things that are dysfunctional, incongruous, and ill-advised. So even if their words contain a grain of truth, the best course of action may be to turn their ideas inside out and upside down. It's not as funny, but it's the preferred plan for growing a healthy marriage.

So again, I hope you didn't detect your husband in too many of those quotations. If you did, take this as a reminder to smile about his shortcomings. For if he's anything like me, they are many.

Besides, a more important question in a book for wives is this: Did you see *yourself* in any of the one-liners above?

Takeaway

Spend enough time celebrating the good stuff in your marriage and you can laugh at the stuff that isn't quite worth celebrating.

"You might not always get what you want, but you always get what you expect."
—CHARLES SPURGEON (1834–1892)

A Husband Needs His Wife…

To Ask the Right Question at the Right Time

Gary and Patty had two promising careers. A solid marriage with two pre-school daughters. And life was good.

One of the unmistakable highlights of Gary's week was playing golf every Saturday. From April through October, if it wasn't thundering and lightning, he was on the course for at least 18 holes. Sometimes the outing included lunch. Once in a while he even played an extra round.

Nothing wrong with that, right? Fresh air. Good exercise. For thousands of men, the weekend round of golf is an American tradition. As long as the girls were little, Patty didn't mind. Hanging out and just being a mom, Patty enjoyed her Saturdays as much or as more than Gary did.

Still, she knew he was missing out. And over the next couple of years, it became clear the girls were missing their dad. A couple of times as Gary was heading out Saturday morning, Patty would drop hints that "today would be a nice family day." Gary heard the words, but he didn't have to think twice. He had already made the commitment. "The guys are expecting me," he'd say. And that's how it went for another week. And another spring, summer, and fall.

The following June, Patty asked the right question at the right time. And she was also ready with the right follow-up response. On a Wednesday evening, she asked her husband, "What are you doing this weekend?"

"I'm playing golf."

"Well, Stephanie has a soccer game and she would love for you to be there. It's actually fun to watch."

To make a long story short, Gary called his golfing buddies and cancelled for that Saturday. He went to his daughter's game and did truly enjoy himself. Just like that, he had a new Saturday tradition. Before long Gary was a soccer coach. And a much more involved father. Telling the tale today, he says, "It changed my life."

Did Patty have a plan? Not really. But she knew her husband well enough to know how he would respond. Naturally, Gary had a loyalty to the other guys in his regular golfing foursome. But Patty knew his real priority was his family.

Patty also knew that nagging or creating a big guilt trip would be counterproductive. But what if Gary had chosen golf over his family? I don't know. There would have certainly been some regrets and other collateral damage along the way.

Looking back, he's grateful for a wife who made the best option clear and gave him time to make the right decision on his own. Nicely done, Patty.

Takeaway

The best way to influence your husband is not to present a persuasive argument that he should take your side, but to let him know you are both already on the same side.

"Give me golf clubs, fresh air and a beautiful partner,
and you can keep the clubs and the fresh air."
—Jack Benny (1894–1974)

A Husband Needs His Wife...

To Do This

I'm going to tuck this little chapter right here about two-thirds of the way through the book. Hiding it so that only committed readers will discover it.

If you've read this far, you know that I am pro-wife and pro-husband and fully realize that the best marriages elevate both him and her. A few paragraphs down, I'm going to give wives a little assignment—a secret—that may very well have more impact than any other advice in the book. It's not an abstract theory, it's something to actually do.

Like most books on family relationships, mine have a good amount of overarching principles. To dads, I'll say you need to "be there" for your kids. Or you need to "enter their world," "build traditions," and "be a hero." Readers will sincerely nod in agreement at such theories and feel good about having acquired some new insight. But the most enthusiastic responses in e-mails, postings, letters, and phone calls describe how a specific recommendation in one of my books or talks—not just a theory—compelled a father to take action. To do something.

"Hey, I built some stilts with my son." "I took Ashley to the daddy-daughter dance." "Jay, I can't believe it, but I cancelled my regular Saturday tee time to coach my kid's soccer team."

In other words, it requires intentionality to move principles from theory to real life. If a father wants to enter his kid's world, build traditions, or be a hero, it takes specific action.

Well, husbands need to feel appreciated and loved. We need to feel important to our wives. More specifically, we need to be affirmed that we're doing a good job as a husband, provider, protector, and lover. Even though our definition is slightly different than yours, men have a legitimate desire for romance. We don't just require an occasional sexual release; we actually want you to want us.

To make it really clear, when we send out our regular hints or direct requests for sex, please don't ignore us or instantly shut us down. You don't need to say yes. (Sometimes you do.) But what's more important is that you acknowledge our desire right then and there and then suggest a timetable. Let us know fairly specifically when you'll be ready for us. Whether that's in the next few hours or the next few days. A flat-out rejection hurts. But a postponement is something we can live with. Actually, it gives us something to look forward to and can even add to the anticipation and enjoyment. Then, of course, you need to keep your promise.

Still, that bit of relationship wisdom is not the secret I promised above. What is that proactive assignment? It's pretty simple. Twice a year initiate sex. Totally out of the blue. Totally unexpected. Send out a clear request to your husband using any signal you want—verbal, nonverbal, or both. If that's something you already do, keep doing it. But probably you are already aware that you are in the minority.

In a strong marriage, nuzzling, cuddling, handholding, and quick smooching are something husbands can expect from their wives. But why don't most women initiate sex? Researchers suggest that some women think it's inappropriate or not their responsibility. Maybe they're afraid of rejection. Which lends a certain irony to the issue. Men also fear rejection, but we take a chance, hoping the rewards outweigh the risk.

A recent study published in the journal *Personality and Social Psychology Bulletin* yielded this surprising conclusion. "The more husbands loved their wives, the *more* likely they were to initiate sex. For wives, though, increased love for their husbands meant they were actually *less* likely to make the first move."[10] So, perhaps, well-loved wives don't feel the need because they already feel cherished and fulfilled. Those women need to know their husband's perspective is exactly the opposite.

If this chapter made you uncomfortable, that may not be a bad thing. If you think the assignment may be meaningful in your marriage, I hope you'll take full advantage.

Finally, we shouldn't leave this topic without confirming there is a flipside. The conventional wisdom that husbands have the more aggressive sexual appetite is not 100 percent accurate. In some marriages, it's just the opposite. Dear reader, if that's the case in your marriage, you may have even picked up this book looking for ways to stir your husband's passions. If I can boil my best advice down to one thought, it would be this. Talk about it. But not in the middle of an argument or frosty standoff. Pick the right day and the right moment and—with grace and humor—help him see the long-term relational benefits of filling each other's most basic needs. Make sense?

Takeaway

Intimacy needs to come from both sides. If you love your husband, let him know.

> *"Some people claim that marriage interferes with*
> *romance. There's no doubt about it. Anytime you have*
> *a romance, your wife is bound to interfere."*
> —GROUCHO MARX (1890–1977)

A Husband Needs His Wife...

To Expect They Will Track with Each Other 78 Percent of the Time

Your husband's passion might be football, model railroading, opera, puppetry, woodcarving, volunteering at Special Olympics, heavy metal bands of the '80s, photography, hockey, magic, archery, spelunking, or triathlons. Whatever it is, I hope there's room for you to join him in pursuing that passionate pastime every once in a while. That's healthy for a marriage.

For the record, my passion is being a dad, and Rita is an awesome partner in parenting. My fourth book, *52 Things Kids Need from a Dad*, became a bestseller because that passion was evident in every page. Because it's good business, my publisher soon suggested some follow-up books.

The day I signed the contract for *52 Things Daughters Need from Their Dads*, a surprising fear swept over me. I knew from personal experience and biblical authority that daughters were different than sons, but I wasn't sure how to say that with authority and conviction. I was well aware that some feminists claim the only reason girls are different from boys is gender stereotyping and environmental influences.

Thinking about boys and girls, maybe they had a point. Kids are a lot alike. Both female and male children need unconditional love, encouragement, instruction, physical challenges, time with Mom, time with Dad, chores, discipline, respect, a sense of right and wrong, a relationship with God, hugs, sleep, birthday parties, bike rides, chocolate-chip cookies, trees to climb, and all kinds of opportunities to explore their world and find their place in it.

On top of those similarities, I ran across a study published in the September 2005 issue of *American Psychologist* magazine. The title of the article by Professor Janet Shibley Hyde of the University of Wisconsin—Madison is "The Gender Similarities Hypothesis."

The 12-page article, which includes two pages of references, several charts and graphs, and lots of big words, is quite impressive. Dr. Hyde looks at a wide variety of personality and cognitive traits, including memory, self-esteem, social behavior, communication, small motor skills, negotiation, smiling, coping, delay gratification, cheating, assertiveness, and anxiety just to name a few. Her conclusion is that 46 meta-analyses confirm that men and women are unequivocally and undeniably very much alike.

However, buried deep in the article is this statement: "78 percent of gender differences are small or close to zero."[11]

Did you get that? Like many studies done in the last half century, the researchers set out to confirm their own agenda. They wanted to prove that there is no difference between boys and girls. After collecting data, they even had the audacity to title their article, "The Gender Similarities Hypothesis." But their own research concludes that girls and boys are *not* the same. Seventy-eight percent of the time they are. But after compiling research from more than 2000 studies, science finally agrees that in 22 percent of the categories, *men and women are significantly different.* Shouldn't that have been the title of the article?

Reviewing the biased media coverage that followed this supposedly groundbreaking 2005 report, the consensus seemed to be that there is zero difference between boys and girls and that parents should be ashamed for treating them differently. Well, science says otherwise.

So—good news for husbands and wives, and boys and girls. It's okay to be different. Women don't need to be ashamed for not appreciating *The Three Stooges* and monster-truck rallies. You may continue to enjoy spinach, get mani-pedis, and visit restaurant lavatories in pairs. Men don't need to be ashamed for falling asleep at symphonies or not knowing the difference between *periwinkle, turquoise,* and *teal.*

I'm probably oversimplifying, but 78 percent of the time you should expect your husband to react like you. Frustration about taxes. Delight in seeing a double rainbow. Sadness when your daughter gets cut from the basketball team. Joy when your son gets into Yale. Fear when you find yourself driving across the state in a sudden ice storm. But the other 22 percent of the time, your husband will respond to a situation quite differently than you.

I'm hoping, of course, you use this data to build a stronger marriage. For the purpose of this book, let's not debate the glass ceiling in the workplace, Title IX, women in combat, and other controversial examples of gender discrimination. Such complex issues cannot be resolved with pithy answers and often need to be considered on a case-by-case basis. But can we at least agree that women and men are different? Which means once in a while you are going to do things that make zero sense to us. And vice versa.

Takeaway

Men's brains are 12 percent bigger than women's brains. Just sayin'.

*"God created mankind in his own image, in the image of God
he created them; male and female he created them."*
—GENESIS 1:27

A Husband Needs His Wife...

To Be Courageous

If you've been reading this book sequentially, you've taken in 36 chapters that hopefully have given you some new insight into your husband and revealed many secrets that will lead to a life together filled with beautiful music and a glowing cascade of syrupy love. Or something like that.

More honestly, you're beginning to realize that there are some things you can change about him and some things you just can't. You bring stuff to the marriage he doesn't. He brings stuff you don't. This thing called marriage is actually a pretty nice little design that serves as a formidable building block for families and communities.

Recent research gathered by the Heritage Foundation confirms that married couples report better health and greater sexual satisfaction, volunteer more, experience less depression, live a more affluent lifestyle, and live longer. Children raised in intact families tend to do better in school, attend church more often, and have fewer emotional problems. In other words, marriage works.[12]

But there are exceptions. And they need to be addressed. The next couple of paragraphs are difficult to write and may be difficult to read.

Because we live in a fallen world, bad stuff happens. When God created the world, he looked around seven different times and said, "This is good" (Genesis 1:4,10,12,18,21,25,31). But then sin entered the world, opening the door to things that were not good. And that includes mental illness, alcohol abuse, abusive backgrounds, addictions, and other personality disorders.

Your husband needs you to stick it out with him through thick and thin. You remember, "To have and to hold, from this day forward, for better, for worse, for richer, for poorer, in sickness or in health, to love and to cherish 'til death do us part." But hear this: That promise you made does not include abuse.

If he physically abuses you, do what you have to do to and get out. I recommend today. If you believe he's being verbally abusive, talk to someone worthy of your trust who can help you sort out his words and threats. If it's abuse, again get out. Marriage is a covenant, and his abuse has broken that covenant. Don't fight back. Don't threaten. Take any kids you have and find safe harbor.

You are not doing him any favors by sticking around. As a matter of fact, your husband needs you to be courageous. He needs you to leave that environment. I'm not recommending divorce. I'm not saying his behavior cannot be changed. The very act of your leaving may be the first step toward healing for that man you love. Once you are physically safe, seek good counsel and God's will. Psalm 32:8 promises, "I will instruct you and teach you in the way you should go; I will counsel you with my loving eye on you."

That's where this chapter has to end. I'm not a psychologist or certified counselor. But I am an advocate for healthy, strong, and lasting marriages. I pray that for yours.

Takeaway

Abuse will harden your heart. You may not see any hope. But marriage should never be tossed aside lightly. Just as it takes courage to leave an unsafe environment, it takes courage to open your heart to the possibility of reconciliation.

> *"The LORD examines the righteous, but the wicked, those*
> *who love violence, he hates with a passion."*
>
> —PSALM 11:5

A Husband Needs His Wife…

To Appoint Him as Project Co-Manager

Here's the scenario. You've got a household project you've been thinking about for months. Maybe years. Something big like remodeling the kitchen or moving to Albuquerque. Or something small like refinishing your grandmother's china cabinet or moving the piano from the family room to the living room. This is something you've been mulling and pondering for so long that you can picture every detail in your head. You are 100 percent sure that completing this project—a project that your husband knows nothing about—would make your life 100 percent better.

Out of the blue, you announce that you're flipping the switch and making it happen. Moving, remodeling, refinishing, making this dream happen is suddenly on the top spot of your to-do list. It's a fast-track project. It's going to happen. And your husband had better get on board or get out of the way.

FYI: When you make your announcement, your husband feels like his life or his weekend has been hijacked by a crazy lady.

It's all news to him. And because he hasn't been given any time to think about it, he's not sure it's a good idea. Or at least he's not sure if you're going about it the right way. Then he makes matters worse by saying something stupid like "What are you talking about?" "That's ridiculous," or "That doesn't make any sense at all." His response is really a defense mechanism because he feels like he has been blindsided.

To be fair, you have been dropping hints for quite a while. But what have you been really saying? You expressed irritation about your dripping kitchen faucet and scratched Formica. You mentioned home prices in Albuquerque.

You fretted that Lysa isn't practicing piano enough because the TV in the family room distracts her.

You think your project should not come as a surprise to your husband. But trust me, it does. Unless you have described it with absolute clarity at a time he was actually listening, he will not waste any brain power on your list of things to do. Your husband has his own list involving big-screen TVs, carburetors, pumpkin catapults, or hunting lodges.

Suddenly, there's a major point of conflict in your marriage and you are darn sure it's all his fault. Maybe it is, maybe it isn't. The real question is, "Where do you go from here?"

Speaking from experience, an eager-to-get-started wife needs to keep a few things in mind. First, there's a high probability your dream project will be completed, so take a breath and please retreat from your attack on your shell-shocked husband. Second, understand that the timetable and scope of the project may change because now you have a partner in the project with his own ideas, priorities, and needs. Third, your husband is also going to bring some "bad news" to the project. He sees things and knows things you don't.

Don't be offended by that—it's just two people with different life experiences. Maybe he knows someone who moved to Albuquerque and hated it. Maybe his mental yardstick knows the piano won't fit where you suggest. Maybe he has his own unspoken plans that totally contradict your unspoken plans.

A recent study comparing the brains of men and women may shed some light. It turns out men use the left side of their brain more (problem-solving, task-oriented), while women use the right side of their brain more (feelings, creativity). Also, men have a thinner parietal region in their brains, which gives them the ability to mentally rotate objects in their mind's eye. That's a blessing and a curse when you start moving furniture and appliances. You tell us something will fit, and we know it won't. Sometimes you're right; usually we are.

In any project you need both vision and execution. You need to invest real money, but you need a budget. You need to get started, but also should have a schedule based on reality. You need the best input of both him and her. Even if you didn't know it, that's one of the reasons you got married. Your best plus his best almost always equals an even better way.

Five real-life lessons learned in more than 30 years of marriage make me an expert on all the above.

Don't buy that van until you see if it fits in the garage.

Don't start the kitchen project two weeks before Thanksgiving.

Don't pull up the carpet until you've priced hardwood floors.

Don't pursue the job in Seattle until you've considered how that might impact your family and extended family.

Don't begin to pull down the drywall until you have a better sense of the sheet-metal ducts and plumbing hidden behind it.

No matter what, trust that in the end it all works out for the best. But once again, the old axioms are proven to be true. Two heads—and two hearts—are better than one.

Takeaway

One-sided decisions might make a house, but they don't make a home. If your husband tells you to go ahead and decorate and remodel any way you want, you'll still want his input. Otherwise, he will always feel like a visitor in his own home.

> *"If you want to make peace with your enemy, you have to work with your enemy. Then he becomes your partner."*
>
> —NELSON MANDELA (1918–)

A Husband Needs His Wife…

To Realize That His Anger Is Not Really Directed at You

This happened last night. True story.

Through her supersonic hearing, Rita hears some clicking coming from the corner of the basement and asks me to check it out. The two of us shuffle down the stairs, sidestepping the plastic tubs overflowing with Christmas decorations, circling around broken window screens and boxes of lightbulbs, and kicking up clouds of sawdust that I should have swept up months ago. The clicking—which I can still barely hear—seems to be coming from the radon abatement unit connected to the sump pump. (Any hassles with that system are a double slap in the face because it was installed to comply with one of those government-mandated health proclamations that always seem like overkill and a scam to middle-class homeowners.)

Rita instructs me that turning the circuit breaker off and on may reboot the system. I dutifully do exactly as I am told. I'm not sure it works, because—again—I can't hear the clicking anyway.

Then, while we're walking past the 26-year-old furnace, Rita notices some water dripping from the humidifier unit. Without a thought, she pops open the front panel and begins to assess the problem. I suggest that it's probably okay, but her body language seems to say that this is another problem that is not going away. Still she's willing to set it aside for now. I watch for 90 seconds or so as she attempts to refasten the front panel of the humidifier. Finally, I take it from her and snap the panel into place.

Most women reading this scenario might applaud Rita for being a conscientious homeowner and eager partner in maintaining our suburban castle on a cul-de-sac. Most men reading this would understand the rage bubbling up from my gut as the two of us trudge back up the stairs.

What could possibly be ticking me off? First, a nice evening interrupted. Second, the possibility of expensive and time-consuming home repairs. Third, an overstuffed basement looking like something out of the reality TV show *Hoarders*. Fourth, the frustration that comes with confronting mechanical systems that are beyond my areas of expertise. Fifth, a wife who doesn't really know how they work either but implies that she does, which makes me feel even more incompetent. Sixth—and this is where the absurdity really sinks in—I'm getting angry that I'm getting angry.

Put another way—I want my wife to see me as the guy who takes care of things. I solve problems in life and around the house. When I can't do that or when she begins to assume that role, I feel somewhat humiliated. It goes along with that desperate need men have for respect from our wives.

What did I do on the way up the stairs? I made things even worse. I said something stupid like, "Next time you take something apart, make sure you can put it back together again." Which left my bride totally confused. Rita had done nothing wrong.

To her credit, she didn't snap back at me. Also to her credit, an hour later when I apologized for being a grump, she didn't pile on.

Finally, when she read the first draft of this chapter minutes ago, she said, "Oh, is that what was going on last night? Jay, I love this house. After all, we raised five great kids here. But I love you more. If a tornado blew down this house tomorrow, it would all work out."

And I said what I always say: "You and me, kid."

Takeaway

Once in a while, you may quite by accident trigger a response from your husband that seems totally out of line. Anger. Regret. Resentment. Stone-cold silence. When that happens, please don't pile on. Also, don't minimize his feelings. If you do insist on discerning the reason for his response, consider how the situation may have left him feeling a little disgraced, humiliated, or ashamed that he couldn't solve a problem that was his responsibility.

"By wisdom a house is built, and through understanding it is established."
—Proverbs 24:3

A Husband Needs His Wife…

To Chase Her Dreams

Follow this fictional scenario: I'm 99 years old, lying in bed and drawing some of my final breaths. My beloved Rita is holding my hand and smiling warmly. She sighs and says, "Thank you, my love, for our wonderful life together." (So far so good. I'm even smiling back.) In the same warm tone she gently adds, "When I think of all the sacrifices I've made and all the dreams I set aside for you and our family, I must say it was almost worth it."

That's when I wake up screaming. I'm pretty sure that scene would be a nightmare for any caring husband. You see, husbands don't want to be the source of any lifelong regrets our wives may have. In the end, men desperately want to look back on our own lives with the satisfaction that we dared greatly and experienced a fair share of triumphs to go along with a handful of well-fought defeats. Even more adamantly, we want to challenge our offspring to reach for still brighter stars. On top of all of that, we want our brides (that's you) to chase and successfully achieve their dreams as well.

The idea that we somehow caused you to abandon your life aspirations creates in us a glut of painful regrets.

Do we expect you to make sacrifices for us? Sure we do. A certain amount of sacrifice is what we both signed up for. It's honorable for husbands and wives to make choices that are best for the entire family. Perhaps it's especially true for women. You may want spinach on your pizza, but your husband and kids thinks green goopy vegetables ruin a perfectly good pie. You want to live in the biggest house in town with a sweeping staircase, a grand solarium, and a full staff of maids, chefs, and gardeners. But you chose to marry for love rather than money. You want to wake up in Paris, but instead you spend your vacation on your in-laws' sofa bed. Indeed, adult life is full of sacrifices.

But trust in this: Your husband really does want you to be happy. As a matter of fact, some of the most heartbreaking moments of a man's life come when he realizes that his wife didn't—or couldn't—experience something she really wanted. Consider these words delivered unexpectedly from loving wife to devoted husband:

"I wish I had gotten my degree."

"I wish we would have had a couple more kids."

"I gave up too soon on my flower shop."

"I wish I had taken better care of myself."

"I should have supported you when you wanted to start your own agency."

"I wish I had invested more in my career."

"I wish I had invested more time in my family."

Heartbreaking words? Perhaps not. If you speak these words with venom as an accusation, such ideas can do great damage. But said thoughtfully to a true partner in life's journey, these may be the first words of a soul-stirring, enlightening, and door-opening conversation.

Be warned. Your courageous statement may take him by surprise. If his initial reaction is not what you had hoped for, please cut him some slack. We're talking about an idea you've been mulling over for years, but it's all news to him. So proceed with caution.

His first response could be confusion: *"What do you mean? You never mentioned this before!"*

It could be an easy answer that is not-so-easy: *"Well, go ahead. No one is stopping you!"*

It could be a welcome invitation: *"Wow. Well, sweetheart, we know that God promises a time for every purpose, and this may be your time."*

If you're real lucky, your husband has already been in tune with your unspoken dreams: *"If it's important to you, it's important to me."*

You probably already have some sense about how your husband will actually respond. Prepare yourself accordingly. You can even show him this chapter and ask him if he wants to know your dreams. You may be launching into one of the most difficult conversations of your life. But in the end, trust that your husband does want to hear any sincere, authentic aspirations you have. And, the sooner the better.

By the way, your husband may also have some hidden hopes and dreams. Go ahead and ask him. But be ready for anything.

Takeaway

In the end, this cannot be about your dreams or his dreams. It needs to be about shared dreams.

"You are never too old to set another goal or dream a new dream."
—C.S. Lewis (1898–1963)

A Husband Needs His Wife…

To Applaud His Tenacious Focus on the Task at Hand

Rita can multitask. I have seen her simultaneously knit, cook dinner, watch TV, entertain the dog, pray for a college-age son traveling cross-country, do laundry, respond to urgent PTO business, tell me about her day, balance the checkbook, and somehow also help me with the one thing I'm trying to do at that moment. I stand in awe of her.

On the other hand, I cannot do more than one thing at a time. Ever. Your husband is the same way. If this is news to you, stop and think about those infuriating moments when you're asking him to do something when he is already doing something.

You're at a local sports-themed restaurant and you're telling him about your sister's new career path, but he doesn't hear you because a playoff game is featured on a big-screen TV over your left shoulder.

His head is in the fridge selecting cold cuts, cheese, pickles, and horseradish for the perfect sandwich, and you dare ask him for the ranch dressing. He closes the door with his elbow carrying an armload of provisions, but no ranch dressing. He either didn't hear or forgot your request.

You set a bag of recyclables by the back door. He walks through that door 17 times while retrieving the right tools to tighten the hub bearing assembly on his 1968 Mustang. The bag of cans, bottles, and cardboard never moves.

You blame him. You may even be angry. But frankly, this is all your fault. Every man I know can only do one thing at a time. Multitasking is totally out of our league. You should know that by now.

Instead of being frustrated, I suggest you choose to marvel at our uncanny ability to focus intently and entirely on one thing at a time. And do it well. In the above examples, your husband knows the Packers were forced to punt because the pulling guard didn't hold his block. That sandwich will be a work of culinary excellence and he may even share it with you. His pride and joy '68 classic car will have the smoothest ride at the next Mustang Road Rally.

By the way, when you do actually get his attention, there's a very good chance your husband will dutifully listen to gossip about your sister, fetch your salad dressing, and adiós the recyclables. The chance will decline if nagging, fuming, or whining enters the picture.

Worth noting—even though your husband can only do one thing at a time, his laser-sharp focus may enable him to achieve multiple goals in the doing.

For example, if he throws himself 100 percent completely into reading a bedtime story to your eight-year-old daughter, he may be achieving more than a half-dozen benefits—long and short term. He's strengthening the family bond and making memories. He's conveying the importance of reading. He's creating a positive experience with your daughter within the walls of her private space, which increases the chance that a parent will be welcome there in the future under more difficult circumstances. Depending on the book, he may be teaching a lesson, sharing a learning experience, or gaining insight into your daughter's world. He's also giving you a little free time for yourself or the other kids. Most importantly, he's setting the mood for a tucking-in prayer and a goodnight hug from his daughter.

All those things happen because he was focusing on the single all-important task of reading a bedtime story to your little girl. Now aren't you glad you married such a high-achievement kind of guy?

So don't make your man feel guilty if he can't multitask. Instead, celebrate his ability to focus on one single thing with complete concentration and laser-like intensity. Even if it's just grilling pork chops, installing a garbage disposal, changing a diaper, or watching football. You can be sure any pursuit he tackles is going to be done with transcendent virtuosity.

———— Takeaway ————

How about this? If you let us go through life the way God wired us, we'll let you go through life the way God wired you. Deal?

> *"Being a woman is a terribly difficult task, since it*
> *consists principally in dealing with men."*
> —JOSEPH CONRAD (1857–1924)

A Husband Needs His Wife...

To Understand the Slippery Slope

This chapter is about porn. And it's not going to be fun to read. But it's a reality that cannot be ignored. According to research from Family Safe Media, 47 percent of marriages in church pews are struggling with pornography. If that's even remotely accurate—and I'm sure it is—then this book would be a sham if it didn't at least address the issue.

Here's the plan. In the next few pages, we're going to look at a few things wives need to know, including a course of action you might want to consider.

First, you need to know that your husband's inclination toward such disturbing images is not your fault. It's not because you're not pretty enough. It's not because he doesn't get enough sex. It's not because he doesn't love you. As the title of the excellent book by Stephen Arterburn and Fred Stoeker suggests, sexual temptation and pornography is *Every Man's Battle*. In other words, virtually every man is on the slippery slope of viewing sexualized images of women. It may sound incongruous, but God designed men with a special receptiveness to visual stimuli. He wanted each man to be enticed and captivated by his one and only, his life companion. But like so many of God's good gifts, it has been terribly misused.

Which leaves your husband fighting a battle against an enemy that is getting stronger every year. I applaud those determined and virtuous men who divert their eyes from a provocative billboard or work hard to not look twice at the curves of a female character in a television sitcom. That's not easy. Conversely, other men have fallen so far that they spend hours every day with images that cannot be described here.

I hope your husband is at the top of that slippery slope. But even then, he is still just a few Internet clicks away from a slide down to the darkness of addiction. And make no mistake, that slide continues to get steeper and faster. Think about how social media like Facebook and Pinterest have become an obsession with some of your female friends. A porn obsession is not as public, but its draw on men is more treacherous, more damaging, and more addictive.

Second, you need to know that there can be victory over any habit or addiction. Including porn. As a matter of fact, there must be victory. For your husband, that victory is between him and God. Alas, you cannot be his rescuer. But as his helpmate, there are things you can do.

- Pray for him. Create an atmosphere for open communication. Don't prod him, but allow him to share his weakness without fear. "Confess your sins to each other and pray for each other so that you may be healed" (James 5:16).

- Strengthen the bond in your family. Help your husband see the rewards of being a faithful husband and father. "The wise woman builds her house, but with her own hands the foolish one tears hers down" (Proverbs 14:1).

- Renew your own commitment to remain faithful. "Marriage should be honored by all, and the marriage bed kept pure, for God will judge the adulterer and all the sexually immoral" (Hebrews 13:4).

- Stick with him. Be a conduit for God's love and faithfulness. "If a woman has a husband who is not a believer and he is willing to live with her, she must not divorce him. For the unbelieving husband has been sanctified through his wife" (1 Corinthians 7:13-14).

- Encourage him to join a men's small group. "If another believer is overcome by some sin, you who are godly should gently and humbly help that person back onto the right path. And be careful not to fall into the same temptation yourself. Share each other's burdens, and in this way obey the law of Christ" (Galatians 6:1-2 NLT)

- Encourage him to meet one-on-one with a godly mentor or accountability partner. "As iron sharpens iron, so one person sharpens another" (Proverbs 27:17).

Still, even with prayer, love, and support from his family and Christian men, your husband has to make that courageous choice himself. Even Job, the Old Testament paragon who "was blameless and upright" and "feared God and shunned evil" (Job 1:1), still had to make an unconditional verbal commitment to God promising he would not sin with his eyes. "I made a covenant with my eyes not to look lustfully at a young woman" (Job 31:1).

Not to oversimplify the entire Bible, but it's really all about having a personal relationship with God. When it comes to how we deal with everything from temptation to salvation, we make our own choice. "We are each responsible for our own conduct" (Galatians 6:5 NLT).

Third, there are proactive ways you can be supportive. I highly recommend the book *For Women Only* by Shaunti Feldhahn. The research and interviews she pulls together will help you understand nine different truths about men that will surely open your eyes. On the topic of how a wife can help her man stay pure in his thought life, Shaunti recalls a helpful acronym:

> Several organizations mention the H.A.L.T. checklist: Hungry, Angry, Lonely, Tired. If a man is working long hours, is out of sorts with the world (or his spouse), feels unappreciated, feels like a failure as a provider, or is far from home on a business trip—if he is hungry, angry, lonely or tired—any of those things could weaken his resolve. If you've ever found yourself eating the entire box of cookies when you're unhappy, you can probably understand this dynamic.[13]

Shaunti also encourages wives to open lines of communication on this very difficult topic. Ask what you can do to help. If your husband confesses his urges and promises to work on turning away from enticing and sensual images, it's okay to show your appreciation. When he *doesn't* track the girl in the revealing outfit or when he *looks away* from the latest Victoria's Secret commercial, go ahead and give him a smile, a squeeze of his hand, or even say, "Thanks for putting me first."

In addition to *For Women Only* and *Every Man's Battle* by Stephen Arterburn and Fred Stoeker, there are quite a few other resources on this topic. Helpful books include *Undefiled* by Harry Schaumburg, *The Bondage Breaker* by Neil T. Anderson, and *Five Steps to Breaking Free from Porn* by

Joe Dallas. Plus, you may want to investigate Christian counselors, support groups and networks, and web filters.

Finally, a word of warning. And this is an unfortunate reality. Some pastors, so-called experts, and books published by reputable authors will suggest that your husband's porn addiction indicates that you're not satisfying his sexual needs. That's just plain wrong. You deserve a husband who certainly can appreciate beauty and has a healthy sexual appetite, but who longs for and desires only you.

Takeaway

If you discover your husband has opened a few websites or paged through a few magazines, please do not give up on him. He needs you more than ever.

> *"Love is a commitment that will be tested in the most vulnerable areas of spirituality, a commitment that will force you to make some very difficult choices. It is a commitment that demands that you deal with your lust, your greed, your pride, your power, your desire to control, your temper, your patience, and every area of temptation that the Bible clearly talks about. It demands the quality of commitment that Jesus demonstrates in His relationship to us."*
>
> —Ravi Zacharias (1946–)

A Husband Needs His Wife...

To Buy Two Jars of Peanut Butter

Oh, the agony of marriage. So often couples bring opposite needs and expectations to their relationship. Drastic incompatibilities clash disastrously delivering devastating and divisive disharmony. What to do? What to do?

She likes coffee; he likes tea. She prefers action movies; he likes romantic comedies. She wants a beach vacation; he wants to take her to a four-star Manhattan hotel. He wants a spruce Christmas tree; she wants a Douglas fir.

It's enough to make you stay single your entire life.

Yes, I know there are different viewpoints and requirements in most marriage relationships. Some might even seem to be deal breakers. But most are not. Most can and should be worked out. And that's the point.

Do you really argue over crunchy versus creamy peanut butter? Buy two jars. Is there debate about who makes the bed? It's the last person up.

Every January, do you clash over the setting on the thermostat? Invest in a cuddly comforter for whichever spouse gets the winter chills.

This is not rocket science, people. It's called life. It's called marriage. None of these differences are worth voting someone off the island. Unsnagging these minor snags just takes a smidge of common sense, a little extra effort, or a dash of compromise.

He flips out when you leave his record collection out of order? Designate a place to set albums aside so he can make sure they're lined up correctly.

You get ticked when he leaves the cap off the toothpaste. Is it really that big a deal?

You prefer Italian food and he prefers Mexican? You probably don't need to hire an attorney to negotiate the details of that peace accord.

Of course, the real topic of this chapter is not about dealing with differences. Differences are the spice of marriage. Your differences were the reason you got married in the first place. What you can't do, he can. And vice versa. You complete each other. The real purpose of this chapter is just to remind you to play nice. When it comes to stupid little quirks and shortcomings, choose to be amused more than annoyed.

If you let them, there are plenty of things that can rob the joy from your day. Some of them you cannot control. But on all those teeny-weeny inconsequential issues, take the easy way out. Laugh them off. Do the easy fix. Find common ground.

On a serious note, there are some issues on which compromise isn't an option. In many marriages, one party might be required or requested to make a huge sacrifice, and that shouldn't be taken lightly. Sometimes a husband or wife needs to set aside his or her *own* needs for the long-term benefit of the *family*. Situations arise: A mandatory cross-country move. A season caring for a loved one. Putting your spouse through med school. Staying home to raise the kids. Months living apart due to military service or career responsibilities. Extended illness. Starting a new business. For the short term, these things will strain even the best marriages. Don't sugarcoat it. Acknowledge the sacrifice. Appreciate the partnership.

But if the biggest frustrations you have in your marriage are about TV remotes, damp towels, dirty dishes, lost car keys, scuff marks on the linoleum, check-engine lights, thermostats, or peanut butter, then you'd better start counting your blessings. You've got a marriage made in heaven.

Takeaway

You know that one silly little issue you nag him about? Today, decide to let it go. You have that power.

"Keep your eyes wide open before marriage, half shut afterwards."
—Benjamin Franklin (1705–1790)

A Husband Needs His Wife...

To Read the Verses That Come Before and After Ephesians 5:22

You can't expect a book like this to skip over Ephesians 5:22: "Wives, submit to your own husbands as you do to the Lord."

For many, it's a troubling or ludicrous command. Cynics quote this verse to prove that the Bible is archaic and irrelevant. A biblically illiterate Neanderthal quotes this verse to keep his wife in a subservient role, insisting her opinion has no value and her contribution to the household is limited to cooking, cleaning, and keeping herself available to his sexual whims. Christian women with husbands who are not church attenders struggle with how to respond to the idea of submission.

Instead of skipping over it, let's put Ephesians 5:22 in context. Upon further examination, I believe you'll discover this verse and its surrounding passages are all about empowerment for every member of the family.

Let's begin with the nine words immediately preceding that verse. Ephesians 5:21 says quite plainly, "Submit to one another out of reverence for Christ." That's pretty clear. The apostle Paul was writing to believers in the church at Ephesus and all believers everywhere. He expected all of us to have the heart of a servant and put first the needs of others.

Then after introducing the concept of submitting to one another, Paul turns his attention to the family, which is the building block of a healthy society. He gives three examples of how submission works in real life for wives, husbands, and kids. Read them for yourself:

Wives, submit to your own husbands as you do to the Lord.

For the husband is the head of the wife as Christ is the head of the church, his body, of which he is the Savior (Ephesians 5:22-23).

Husbands, love your wives, just as Christ loved the church and gave himself up for her...In this same way, husbands ought to love their wives as their own bodies. He who loves his wife loves himself (5:25,28).

Children, obey your parents in the Lord, for this is right (6:1).

Men, women, and children have different needs, so Paul explains how to honor and affirm each of them differently. Children need instruction. Women need to feel cherished. Men need to lead.

Submission is all about putting the needs of other members of your family ahead of your own. But today's culture doesn't place a very high value on others. Selfishness, misplaced priorities, and exhaustion keep us from nurturing our own submissive hearts and we have nothing left to give to the people we love most.

- Busy parents sometimes don't have the time or energy to instruct and discipline their kids, but that's what they need. Our kids are counting on us to teach them right from wrong.

- Distracted husbands sometimes forget to do the little things (and the big things) to express love to our wives. But a husband's sacrificial love for his bride is critical for a healthy marriage.

- Exhausted wives sometimes make family decisions without any input from their husbands. She's trying to manage a household and can't even get his attention. He feels out of the loop and the family loses his leadership. And he loses their respect.

Can you see the immediate benefits of Ephesians chapter 5 to both a wife and husband? Some theologians call it "mutual submission." Others don't like that term, but it's a pretty accurate paraphrase of how the Bible describes a successful marriage. He feels respected. She feels loved. Both are looking for the best in each other and looking out for each other.

So next time you hear someone misquote Ephesians 5:22, you are now equipped to get in his or her face and say, "You know, I think you're taking that verse out of context. Have you even read that complete passage of the Bible?"

────────── **Takeaway** ──────────

Any discussion about mutual submission must include the mandate of Genesis 2:24, "And they become one flesh." When you're looking out for your spouse, you're really looking out for yourself. And vice versa.

> *"There is nothing more admirable than two people who see eye-to-eye keeping house as man and wife, confounding their enemies, and delighting their friends."*
>
> —HOMER (NINTH CENTURY BC)

A Husband Needs His Wife…

To Forgive Him at the First Hint of an Apology

We know we mess up more than you. Hey, we're guys. We're risk takers. We sometimes act before considering the consequences of our actions. We speak before thinking about the repercussions of our words. This should not come as a surprise to you.

What you may not know is this. When we mess up, nine times out of ten we know it instantly. It may appear as if we're oblivious to our transgressions. Often we may not acknowledge it immediately. We may strategically wait and see how the sequence of events plays itself out before deciding what our next step should be. Hey, maybe no one noticed, and there's always a chance the damage will disappear on its own. But for the most part we are pretty good at self-policing our actions. Which means we don't need you to point out every mistake every time we make one. And we don't need you to hold a grudge once we begin to make amends.

An example: Let's say your husband gets absorbed in the second overtime of a critical 49ers game and therefore doesn't get to the hardware store before closing, which means he doesn't replace the dimmer switch for the dining-room chandelier as he had promised. When the game is over and he walks past the dining room, he instantly remembers his promise and feels huge amounts of regret, remorse, and self-loathing. But he also knows it's not the end of the world. Your upcoming dinner party is still two weeks away. He considers his calendar for the week and makes a mental note to tackle the project on Thursday night. A few minutes later you walk in the door. Even before your homecoming, you were fairly certain he hadn't replaced that dimmer switch.

More than once before he had promised to do something on a Sunday afternoon, but got distracted by televised sports. The stage is set for an unpleasant standoff, which will lead to a frosty Sunday evening and a hostile beginning to the week. Yikes.

Truthfully, your husband actually does feel a little bad and decides to deliver a preemptive apology. He knows if you speak first—"Did you replace that dimmer switch?"—then his fate is sealed. But if he can offer a quick, sincere apology, there's a chance to rescue the evening. "Hey, Sweetheart. I feel bad, I didn't get to the hardware store for the dimmer switch…"

Wives, you have essentially two choices. Maybe three.

One choice is to jump down his throat, using your steel-vault recollection of all his past nonachievements. You raise your voice: "Again! Remember the garage-door opener? Remember the dripping faucet? Remember the lawn gnome? Every time I ask you to do something, I have to remind you a dozen times." Wives, if that accusatory tone sounds familiar, then you need to considering backing off and toning down.

A second choice is to totally let him off the hook. Without a hint of sarcasm, you could say, "No problem. Really, there's no hurry. And, you know what dear? If you can't get to it before the dinner party, well then somehow we'll survive with lights that can't be dimmed." Now you might think he would appreciate being let off the hook, but actually he doesn't want to hear those words with that tone either. Your husband doesn't want a complete pardon of his sin. He wants to even the score (in a good sense). Men expect to be held accountable. But we also expect the punishment to fit the crime.

So is there a better choice? I think it looks and sounds something like this. You wrap your arms around his neck—hugging, not choking—and say, "You rotten, lazy, no good son-of-a-gun. Just for that, you're going to have to take me out for dinner tonight." Or you might say, "No worries. But there are three or four more things that need to get done before the dinner party. Just letting you know."

The idea is this. When your husband truly apologizes, don't make him squirm even more. Don't rant, but don't completely let him off the hook. Accept his apology, but slap him with just enough of a sentence that he feels like he has paid the price and you're once again even.

Worth noting: Your husband's apologies may not always include the words "I'm sorry" or "I apologize," but you should know him well enough to get his signal and then turn effectively from accuser to supportive wife.

One other warning. All of the above really applies to minor infractions. In a marriage, if one of you does something truly hurtful, then it can't and shouldn't be brushed away. There needs to be a sincere apology that includes an acknowledgment of the hurt. Plus, some kind of willingness to make amends. Then it's really up to the offended spouse to extend grace. All of which may take some time, days even.

Anytime wives and husbands disappoint each other, the goal is reconciliation. If it's a reoccurring character flaw or deliberate cruelty, then I encourage you to pursue some help beyond anything found in this chapter or even this book. An apology is a good start, but it's only the first step toward repentance, repair, and restoration.

But if your husband's biggest wrongdoing is something minor like forgetting to pick up the dry cleaning or being distracted by a football game, you may want to count your blessings and make the punishment something you can both enjoy. You should still expect an apology. But I'm thinking the penalty for tracking mud on your carpet might be dinner and a movie. Leaving the milk out overnight might be Starbucks lattes to go. And leaving whiskers in the sink might be giving you a back rub or foot massage.

Takeaway

Only husbands and wives who are perfect can do marriage without learning the art of asking and giving forgiveness. All others must practice, practice, practice.

> *"Be kind and compassionate to one another, forgiving each other, just as in Christ God forgave you."*
> —Ephesians 4:32

A Husband Needs His Wife...

To Know a Few Other Secrets That Didn't Qualify for an Entire Chapter

There are many things your husband wants you to know, but he is too shy to say or a little embarrassed about. Or maybe he doesn't know that you don't know. Keep a bookmark in this page for future reference.

- We're more like puppy dogs than you think. We'll follow you around hoping for a little attention.

- We like when you put on our clothes. Especially dress shirts.

- Very often we wonder how we got so lucky. How someone amazing like you married a guy like us.

- When we buy flowers, it really is a big deal. We don't mind flowers, but we don't see the value in them. Flowers on a table, we typically don't even notice. So when we buy them, we are really doing a totally selfless act.

- When we cook, it also is a really big deal. At least we think it is. If we flip some burgers, put a frozen pizza in the oven, or whip up some mac and cheese, we expect you to be eternally grateful. Of course, it's not really a big deal. But you need to know that we think it is.

- We also think it's a big accomplishment when we load the dishwasher, vacuum a single room, or do a load of laundry. "Look, dear, aren't I awesome?"

- We like it when your nails look nice. Not too long, but nicely manicured. If it doesn't break the budget, we even like that it cost $40. Even if you paid for it, pretend that we paid for it. It makes us feel like we bought you a gift and didn't have to shop or wrap anything.

- We don't get jealous if you point out how cute a movie star is. He's on a two-dimensional screen and we're right next to you. We win!

- We really don't know what to get you for your birthday, so drop lots of hints. It's really okay.

- We like bacon. Although that's not really a secret, is it?

- If you're dragging us to a social event, as we enter go ahead and say, "You look good in that suit." We'll enjoy the evening ever so much more.

- We never ignore you intentionally. Your voice may have been loud enough to penetrate our inner ear, but it didn't make it through to our cerebrum. Whatever we were focusing on was *not* more important than you. But it had our attention first, so we missed what you said. If it was important (and I'm sure it was), please repeat it without getting angry.

- If we think it's important, we can learn and change. But positive reinforcement works tons better than negative consequences.

- We're not psychic. You may have dropped ten thousand hints, but sometimes you need to come right out and tell us what you want. Yes, we should have thought of it ourselves, but we didn't. Whatever it is, we want you to have it...that is, if you really want it.

- When you say, "That's fine," we think you mean that something is okay. We don't know that when you say, "That's fine," you really mean it is not okay. Just so you know. Okay?

- We have favorite meals. We love it when you take the time and effort to prepare them for us. It's really true that "the way to a man's heart is through his stomach."

- Even when we're studying a spreadsheet, engrossed in the last seconds of a basketball game, pounding the keyboard on a deadline, or even on the phone with our biggest client, we love it when you come up behind us, wrap your arms around our shoulders, and nuzzle our neck.

- We like how you smell. After a shower. All dressed up. Or after working in the garden.

Allow me to end this chapter with a list of the four basic marital needs of all husbands, from the outstanding book by Jimmy Evans, *Lifelong Love Affair.* If you read this list to your husband he would say that those four needs are obvious no-brainers. But in his counseling, Jimmy has found that many of the wives in struggling marriages are either totally surprised by the needs on this list or they totally downplay their importance:[14]

1. Husbands need to feel honored and respected by their wives.

2. Husbands need sexual intimacy.

3. Husbands need friendship—a wife who enjoys doing fun things together.

4. Husbands need domestic support—a wife who takes care of the home.

So now you know some secret needs of men and some needs that are not so secret. You have no more excuses for pleading ignorance.

By the way, you can share the list of *your* needs with *us* anytime. But make sure you get our attention first. Because we really do want to hear specific instructions on how to make you happy.

Takeaway

Much has been written about the mystery of what women want. This is one of the few places you'll find an entire chapter devoted to what men want. You're welcome.

"Husbands are like fires. They go out when unattended."

—Zsa Zsa Gabor

A Husband Needs His Wife…

To Get on the Same Page

A friend of mine can pinpoint the exact moment when his marriage turned from two people who happened to be raising a family together to a true partnership. Which, of course, is a good thing. But for a brief moment, it was not pleasant. Not pleasant at all.

For the first years of marriage, my friend and his bride did what all couples do. They began to establish preferences and priorities. They made some decisions together and some independently. After a few years, the picture of their shared life began to unfold and their individual true colors started to become clear.

Now, if you've married someone much like yourself, then maybe you already live on the same page. Any necessary adjustments are minor. But if you and your husband are living proof that "opposites attract," then maybe you both need to get off the page marked "me" and come together on the page marked "us."

In truth, most marriages will require a certain number of sacrifices and compromises. The two of you may have generated enough different pages to fill an encyclopedia—where to live, where to vacation, how many cars, how many kids, how often to have sex, who controls the remote, cats versus dogs, Macs versus PCs, where to celebrate holidays, should the toilet paper roll dispense over or under, and so on. As you can see, some decisions are monumental. Others not so much.

You won't be surprised to hear that experts say "finance" is the number-two cause of marital discord. It doesn't matter how much money is coming in. There always seem to be unexpected expenses that blow the budget (if there is a budget). And there's quite often a difference of opinion about what's important. All of us like to keep up with the Joneses. Some of us, unfortunately, feel like we need to keep *ahead* of the Joneses.

Frugal versus prodigal. It's a classic marital clash. Sometimes the arguments about money are loud and frequent. Sometimes—and maybe this is even worse—opinions on financial priorities remain unspoken and hidden just below the surface.

After about seven years of marriage, such was the case with my friend and his wife. Oddly enough, it was during a season of life in which the monthly bills were mostly getting paid. The family budget was actually working. But both wife and husband had a sense something was missing. Both were working full-time. He was working on his MBA. The kids' schedules were getting busier. And both he and she knew something had to change.

It's unclear who spoke first. Maybe—like on a TV sitcom—they both spoke at the same time. She said she wanted to turn life up a notch with a bigger house and fancier vacations, which would require more income. In the same instant, he said he wanted to cut back on expenses and maybe even downsize in order to simplify their life. This husband and wife were both responding with honesty and sincerity. From different pages. It got loud. But just for a moment.

He left the room. "I'm done," he said.

What those two words meant exactly was never revealed. Before that moment, she had not known how he felt. He had been feeling stressed and under pressure for quite some time, but he had hidden it well. Perhaps too well. To her great credit, this thirtysomething wife responded with sensitivity, wisdom, love, and trust. In a stunningly short time, that entire family shifted their focus from looking inward to looking out.

A new story was being written. That day of reckoning that could have driven them apart had driven them together. You won't be surprised to hear that God—who had been relegated to an occasional guest in their home—was soon given ownership of all they had. And he gave back a hundredfold.

That wife and husband have been on the same page in the book of life ever since.

Takeaway

Being on the same page is often about finances, but there are so many other challenges you may face. Almost every couple will come to a defining moment when one of you needs to have the courage to say, "It cannot go on like this." And the other needs to have to courage to say, "Let's face this together." I pray you'll be ready for that defining moment in your marriage. Expect it.

> *"Make my joy complete by being of the same mind, maintaining*
> *the same love, united in spirit, intent on one purpose. Do nothing*
> *from selfishness or empty conceit, but with humility of mind*
> *regard one another as more important than yourselves."*
> —Philippians 2:2-3 nasb

A Husband Needs His Wife...

To See the Seasons

On October 31, 2010, our alderman walked down the street and rang our doorbell. Betsy wasn't trick-or-treating. (Actually it turned out she was both tricking and treating, although that wasn't her intention.) After six terms as alderman for the Second Ward, Betsy was stepping down. The next election was five months away, and she had come to our house seeking just the right person to replace her on the city council.

Betsy had talked to several constituents. She had prayed about the right person to approach. And the same name kept coming up. (Not mine. I would be a lousy civil servant or politician.) Betsy came to our house that day to invite, urge, cajole, and challenge Rita to run for alderman.

It had never occurred to my wife to enter politics. She had served as president of the PTO at two local schools and as president of the local high-school athletic booster club. As a caring mom of five active public-school kids, Rita regularly found herself invited to join panels and advisory groups for school boundaries and curriculum issues. In a Chicago suburb of 35,000 where commuters frequently move in and out, Rita and I were fixtures. We were high-school sweethearts who still lived in the same town in which we fell in love. And we loved St. Charles as well.

Rita got my full support. Together we ran a competent and efficient campaign against an entrenched opponent. I helped write letters, postcards, and even some candidate position statements. We stumped through the surrounding neighborhoods and erected a trunk full of yard signs that said "Vote Rita Payleitner Second Ward Alderman." Four newspapers covered the campaign. And she won a very, very close race.

So then what? What started as a whim was suddenly a weekly or even daily responsibility. Since that spring election, my alderman wife has attended three to eight meetings every week. That includes city council, city planning, arts council, historical society, and Kiwanis, as well as all the planning and committee meetings that lead up to those larger meetings. Plus, hours of research, e-mails, and phone conversations.

So where does that leave husband Jay? Sometimes I'm a bit lonely feeling outside the loop, pecking away on my MacBook Pro while Rita "has a city to run." Sometimes I'll escort her on city business as she surveys a piece of property or dedicates a new construction project. Sometimes I'll even throw on a sport coat to be charming arm candy at a fundraiser, dedication, or grand openings. And I haven't missed a parade yet, waving and whistling at the city council float.

This has been a totally unexpected season in our lives. Amusing. Constructive. Revealing. Surprising. Nationally, I'm a bestselling author. Locally, I'm the alderman's husband. Neither of those titles were on anyone's radar screen when we walked down the aisle.

The lesson here is this. Wives (and husbands), I urge you to make the most of every season in your married life. They all come with their own joys and frustrations, responsibilities and surprises, blessings and sorrows, beginnings and ends.

If the honeymoon is barely over and you're wondering what happened to that handsome, attentive, and generous fiancé, give him time. He's wondering a few things too.

If you're up to your armpits in baby drool, soccer schedules, broken appliances, and bad-hair days, please remember that this exhausting season doesn't last forever. You'll miss it more than you could ever imagine. (Take lots of photos.)

Maybe you're courageously enduring a season of true agony. You have a teenager heading the wrong direction. Illness or loss has brutalized your family. Maybe you can't even identify the problem, but a dark cloud has settled over your home. You may need some professional help to guide you into a brighter season, and that's okay too. Every spring begins in winter.

For Rita and Jay, we were just getting used to the idea of sending our youngest child off to West Point when the alderman down the street knocked on our door. We had been wondering how we would survive an empty nest life with much less to do and more time on our hands. That season of idleness never happened. But it still might—only God knows.

Oh yeah, even as this book goes to press, we're expecting our first grandchild. Yet another season. Yay!

Takeaway

Don't disregard any of your life experiences. God will use them all. The relationships you've built. The lessons you've learned. The sacrifices, setbacks, and detours along the way. Who you have become is the person God will use in your next season of life.

"Winter was nothing but a season of snow; spring, allergies; and summer...It was the worst. That was swimsuit season."

—Teresa Lo

A Husband Needs His Wife…

To Play Hard-to-Get

Remember dating? You were the prize, and he played the game to win your affection. It was all so innocent and fun. You flirted a little, but not too much. That initial boy-girl attraction left you and him a little breathless. Maybe not right away, but at some point you both thought, *Could this be the one?*

In the old days, your first connection would have been eye contact across a classroom, at your place of work, or a casual meeting through a friend of a friend. In recent years, your first interaction might have been online in some chat room or Facebook connection. No matter, there was an attraction. You liked his sideways sense of humor, his sturdy jawline, or his twinkly puppy-dog eyes. I invite you, right now, to think about that moment, that give-and-take between you and your future husband.

Where did it go from there? Part of you wanted to move things along, but something told you to slow down and get to know this character before acting too impulsively. You sent out a batch of signals. He picked up on some. He missed some too. You realized that telepathy does not work, so you became a little more obvious. If you didn't know, he was just as nervous as you. Go ahead and ask him to recall those tantalizing moments of your early courtship.

From here at my keyboard, I would not dare judge your first kiss. It might have been electric. Or not. For Rita and me it was a single short kiss on her front porch at the end of our first official date. It left me with a smile and a bunch of unanswered questions. It was early spring in my senior year of high school; she was a year younger. Who could have seen the future back then? Only God.

I would not be surprised if your first kiss with your future husband was also on a first or second date. That seems to be the American way. If you grew up in a more conservative home, it might have taken several dates or a serious commitment from your admirer. For some that first kiss may have come early and opened a floodgate of smooching that I hope didn't go too far too soon.

One of the things men like best is the chase. The quest. In the early days of a relationship, couples are eager to listen and learn about each other. Of course, his motives are different than hers. She's trying to discern whether or not he will be a good friend, father, provider, and partner. He, on the other hand, is trying to figure out what she likes and how he can persuade her to let down her guard. He's trying to get to the next level of romantic interplay.

When he sends his cleverest signals, she may ignore them or miss them entirely. But the most fun is when she receives those signals loud and clear, but pretends not to. It's not a tease. It's not mean. It doesn't cause him to rev his engines and then slam on the brakes. (Always frustrating, if you didn't know.) What she is saying is, "Hey, buddy. I am interested. You have my full attention. But be patient, because I am worth the wait." If he's the right guy for this gal, he knows this is all just part of the chase.

Which leads to this important side note. Premarital sex pretty much eliminates this wonderful romantic courtship. And that's a real loss for any couple. Going too far too soon shuts down all that great interaction and illumination. She never gets a chance to gather all the information she needs about her possible future husband. And he never learns how to truly romance his bride or how to be patient—a skill that's necessary for all good husbands. Instead of trying to figure out each other, sexually active unmarried couples spend all their time trying to figure out when they're next going to have sex.

If you slept together too soon, you may want to make up for some of the missed courtship by intentionally sharing more of your hopes and dreams and telling him you'd like to be wooed. (I'd love to hear his reaction to that request.) Or even ask this question, "Do you think we slept together too soon? What if I would have made you wait?" Don't expect a serious answer. He'll probably say something like, "Oh, I would've dumped you and married (fill in the name of an ex-girlfriend)."

In every good marriage, I believe the game—the flirtations, the secret signals, the promise—builds anticipation and makes sex better. There are exceptions. You have to study each other and know what works and what doesn't. Of course, spontaneity is almost always well-received by a husband.

But never doubt the power of anticipation. That could mean promising sex this afternoon, tonight, or this weekend in a whisper, a note, a cryptic text, an asterisk on a calendar, or a sly glance that only he recognizes at an evening gathering. Or it could be that provocative game of playing hard-to-get. Just as long as you eventually allow him to capture the prize.

Takeaway

Sex is God's gift to married couples. Open it. Enjoy it.

"You'll be happy if you'll remember that men don't change much. Women do. Women adapt themselves, and if you think that means they lose their individuality, you're wrong. Show me a happy marriage and I'll show you a clever woman."

—Elizabeth Cadell (1903–1989)

A Husband Needs His Wife...

To Treasure the Traditional Roles

Writing this book I've been very careful—maybe too careful—to avoid some of the husband-wife stereotypes. Man as exclusive breadwinner. Woman as exclusive homemaker. I am well aware that quite a few couples turn that tradition upside down.

The Bureau of Labor Statistics reports that among "dual-career couples, wives earned more than their husbands 28.9 percent of the time."[15] And according to the U.S. Census Bureau, "Fathers are the primary caregivers for about a quarter of the nation's 11.2 million preschoolers whose mothers work." For better or worse, roles are blurring.

Still, I hope you'll agree that there's something honorable about the idea of a man working hard to give his wife and kids a nice home, pay the bills, and take a family vacation once or twice a year. If you didn't know, you should probably be aware that men have frail egos and a great deal of pride tied up in our ability and need to provide for our family. That's a big deal to us. Even Christian men, who have their identity rooted in Christ, have a huge part of our self-worth tied up in our role as breadwinners. Wives, if your salary provides more than or close to 50 percent of the household income, your husband sometimes feels like a little less of a man. Really. Just ask him.

Even though I've provided 90 percent of our family income for three decades, I experienced that feeling of failure firsthand. As our youngest approached her last year of high school, Rita was offered a part-time job at church. The extra income helped our cash flow, but I'm still surprised at how that made me feel like I wasn't living up to my responsibilities. You can call me old-fashioned, but the Bible backs me up: "If anyone does not provide for his own, and especially for those of his household, he has denied the faith and is worse than an unbeliever" (1 Timothy 5:8 NASB).

Wives and husbands, please don't restructure your entire family financial planning and career goals because of this little chapter. But do recognize that if most husbands were designing the ideal division of duties, they would want to be the ones working hard on the job while their wives were keeping the home fires burning brightly. (Notice I never suggested anything about wearing aprons or pearls. Or having his pipe and slippers ready at the door when he came home.)

A great way to end this chapter might be to throw out a few things you actually can do once in a while that will make your man feel cherished, appreciated, and appropriately masculine no matter who brings home the biggest paycheck.

In no particular order: *Make him his favorite meal once in a while. Let him open your car door. Let him kill spiders and other creepy-crawlies. Let him control the remote. Sit on his lap. Arrange for dinner by candlelight. Bake some cookies. Interrupt his lawn mowing with a glass of lemonade. Put a note in his lunch. Kiss him for 15 seconds. Ask him to open a jar. Ask him to smell your new perfume. Wake him up to investigate the spooky sound you heard in the basement. Put your hand on his chest and feel his heartbeat. Tell him he's more handsome now then on your wedding day.*

The most amazing part of a list like this is that you already knew all this. And you could add a dozen more items. You just needed to give yourself permission to follow through. Well, permission granted.

Takeaway

The culture may change. The traditions may change. Even the rules may change. But a man will always need to feel respected and appreciated. And the best person to do that is his bride.

> *"There is no more lovely, friendly, and charming relationship, communion, or company than a good marriage."*
> —Martin Luther (1483–1546)

A Husband Needs His Wife…

To Give Him Credit

At least once a month I'll tell someone that, "If it wasn't for Rita, I'd be living in a van down by the river." It always gets a laugh. But it's especially funny because it's based on a kernel of truth.

No doubt, our lives are a product of two partners working side by side, interdependent on each other's strengths and filling in the gaps for each other's weaknesses. Rita and I count on each other. But I am not exaggerating when I say I would be a lesser man without her. Maybe I wouldn't be living in my car in a flood zone, but I am going to give her…umm…82 percent of the credit for our comfy home and awesome kids.

One of the ways Rita pours into my life is through words of affirmation. Somehow she knows exactly what I need to hear and when I need to hear it. One of the best examples of that goes back a few years, and I suggest it to any wife who wants to give an incredible (and affordable) gift to her husband.

Rita came close to me and simply said, "I love my life." Wow. Remembering that moment and typing those words warms my toes.

Those words weren't spoken after an amazing sequence of perfect days. That would have been too easy.

Those words weren't spoken in the midst of a cruel season of suffering and setbacks. That would have been too hard to believe.

As I recall, Rita delivered those four kind and loving words in the middle of a period of relative comfort. Not too high. Not too low. She didn't gush with over-the-top praise. Nor was she trying to charm me into some household project or shopping trip. It was an authentic and sincere moment. A moment my mind has come back to dozens of times. Especially when I'm lacking a little confidence or suffering from a binge of self-doubt.

And that's the point. Guys need to be affirmed. We need to know our efforts are meeting and exceeding expectations at home, on the job, in any and every battlefield, and in the bedroom. Especially with you, our helpmate and soul mate who knows us better than anyone. When our careers are crumbling, we need to know you trust us to provide. When the precocious children down the street are getting trophies, blue ribbons, and college scholarships, we need to know our kids are turning out just fine, thank you. When life is passing by, we desperately need to hear that you "love your life."

Now I know we need to be careful here. Some might say that it's not biblical to "love your life." In John 12:25, Jesus even says, "Anyone who loves their life will lose it." And the truth is, if this life on this earth is your only reality, then you're in deep weeds. But if you have secured an eternal home in heaven, then you have a responsibility to live an abundant life that reflects that hope.

So, I sincerely hope you're in a spot where you can say, "I love my life," as well as, "I'm looking forward to loving my life in glory." Say either or both of those phrases to your husband and you're telling him that he's doing a pretty good job as husband, father, provider, and spiritual head of the family.

There's a good chance your words may even motivate him to work a little harder on behalf of your shared life. Well-chosen words can have that kind of impact.

Takeaway

Your husband longs to hear you say that he's doing a good job. Don't worry that he'll take your compliment and suddenly bask in his achievements and get all lazy. Your words of appreciation will actually have the opposite effect.

"The thief comes only to steal and kill and destroy; I came that they may have life, and have it abundantly."

—John 10:10 nasb

A Husband Needs His Wife...

To Trust Love

Are you afraid of falling out of love with your husband?

Don't be. As a matter of fact, instead of being afraid, do just the opposite. Expect it. Anticipate it. Plan for it. Know that sometime down the road, if you haven't already, you're going to look at your husband and think, *Where's the love? Who is this person I'm married to? What's missing?*

As terrifying as that sounds, you need to trust love. Trust that in the very near future, the entire emotional tidal wave of feelings we equate with love will once again wash over you and that man who asked you to marry him. And the fear will be gone. Until next time.

When the feeling comes that you are "falling out of love," the absolute worst thing you can do is panic. When you panic, you do things you regret later. You say things that hurt and, unfortunately, continue hurting your husband even after the gooshy love feelings come back. Your imagination takes an unfortunate turn, nurturing a fantasy life that doesn't include your husband. Online, you search names of old boyfriends. Instead of just smiling at the delivery guy, you start to flirt—just a little. Romance novels gain a new appeal.

Wives who fail to trust love are an obvious target audience for the hugely popular *Fifty Shades of Grey* trilogy and the many spinoffs, sequels, and derivative novels marketed to women depicting lengthy and graphic sex scenes. That's dangerous territory.

Instead of turning your imagination loose, consider how much you have to lose. Your husband is missing you as much as or more than you are missing him. Please don't put up a barrier between yourself and the one person who also is afraid, who also wants to feel love again.

While panic brings trouble and regret, patience brings hope. Trust the power of love to do what it does best. You've read it before, but take a fresh look at 1 Corinthians 13. Instead of a list of instructions, this time see the passage as a promise.

> Love is patient, love is kind. It does not envy, it does not boast, it is not proud. It does not dishonor others, it is not self-seeking, it is not easily angered, it keeps no record of wrongs. Love does not delight in evil but rejoices with the truth. It always protects, always trusts, always hopes, always perseveres. Love never fails (1 Corinthians 13:4-8).

Did you see it? Did you see that love has inherent staying power?

You can trust love to protect and persevere. As long as you and your husband have not given up, love will not fail. It might not *feel* like it, but love is still there. It may feel like you're drifting further apart or are stuck in some kind of desolate wasteland, but when you come out on the other side, love will be stronger, deeper, and more passionate than ever.

Taking one step back in order to take three steps forward is not unprecedented. The science of athletic training dictates that muscles must be broken down to come back stronger. Artists who have lost their passion go back to the basics of painting still life. When the ballet troupe reconvenes to begin rehearsal for their new season, the artistic director emphasizes fundamentals—the plié, tendue, balance, attitude, pointe work. Veteran performers actually look forward to starting from the basics each year.

So instead of panicking, consider going back to the basics. Spend time together. Do what friends do. Do what lovers do. Talk it out. Remember the past. Envision the future. You didn't always love each other, but you grew into love.

There's a great quote from Anne Meara of the comedy team Stiller and Meara. She was responding to a question about her decades-long marriage to Jerry Stiller: "Was it love at first sight? It wasn't then—but it sure is now."

Your wedding vows were really a public commitment to trust love. In any given season—especially during the years when careers are being built, kids are requiring constant attention, and exhaustion rules the day—it may be difficult to even remember that feeling of first love. Be patient. There will come a time when you once again see your husband across a crowded room and your heart will say, "There he is. There's my love."

Takeaway

Feeling in love is fantastic. Being in love is even better.

> *"One advantage of marriage, it seems to me, is that when you fall out of love with each other, it keeps you together until maybe you fall in love again."*
> —JUDITH VIORST (1931–)

Notes

1. "Divorce begets divorce but not genetically," Indiana University press release, July 10, 2007, http://newsinfo.iu.edu/news/page/normal/5982.html.

2. Respectively: Sara McLanahan and Gary Sandefur, *Growing Up with a Single Parent: What Hurts, What Helps* (Harvard University Press, 1994); Deborah A. Dawson, "Family Structure and Children's Health and Well Being: Data from the National Health Interview Survey on Child Health," *Journal of Marriage and the Family* 53 (1991); Peter Hill, "Recent Advances in Selected Aspects of Adolescent Development," *Journal of Child Psychology and Psychiatry* 34 (January 1993), 69-99; Wade Horn and Andrew Bush, "Fathers, Marriage, and Welfare Reform," Hudson Institute Executive Briefing (Indianapolis, IN: Hudson Institute, 1997).

3. Sheila Wray Gregoire, *31 Days to Great Sex* e-book (2012; sold by Amazon Digital Services).

4. Joke borrowed by the author from the highly recommended Good Clean Funnies List at GCFL.net.

5. Annie Chapman, *The Mother-In-law Dance* (Eugene, OR: Harvest House Publishers, 2004), 86, 93.

6. Luke 1:38 GNT.

7. www.prnewswire.com/news-releases/moms-aspire-to-be-modern-day-june-cleavers-according-to-a-new-women-at-nbcu-study-which-paints-a-dramatically-altered-picture-of-todays-american-family-131020118.html.

8. www.prnewswire.com.

9. www.sleepfoundation.org/sleep-topics/napping.

10. www.medicaldaily.com/articles/11197/20120731/love-marriage-men-women-affection-relationship.htm, emphasis (italics) added by author. Also http://health.usnews.com/health-news/news/articles/2012/07/31/love-knows-no-gender-difference?page=2.

11. Janet Shibley Hyde, "The Gender Similarities Hypothesis," *American Psychologist*, Sept. 2005, 581-592.

12. www.familyfacts.org/briefs/1/the-benefits-of-marriage; www.familyfacts.org/briefs/6/benefits-of-family-for-children-and-adults.

13. Shaunti Feldhahn, *For Women Only* (Colorado Springs, CO: Multnomah, 2006), 133.

14. Jimmy Evans, *Lifelong Love Affair* (Grand Rapids, MI: Baker Books, 2012), 109.

15. Bureau of Labor Statistics, *Women in the Labor Force: A Databook: 2011*, "Table 25: Wives Who Earn More Than Their Husbands, 1987-2009" (2011).

Books by Jay Payleitner

Once Upon a Tandem

The One-Year Life Verse Devotional

52 Things Kids Need from a Dad

365 Ways to Say "I Love You" to Your Kids

52 Things Wives Need from Their Husbands

One-Minute Devotions for Dads

If God Gave Your Graduation Speech

52 Things Daughters Need from Their Dads

52 Things Husbands Need from Their Wives

About the Author

Jay Payleitner is a dad. But he pays his mortgage and feeds his family working as a freelance writer, ad man, motivational speaker, and radio producer with credits including *Josh McDowell Radio*, *WordPower*, *Jesus Freaks Radio*, and *Today's Father with Carey Casey*. Jay served as the Executive Director for the Illinois Fatherhood Initiative and is a featured writer/blogger for the National Center for Fathering. He is the author of the bestselling *52 Things Kids Need from a Dad*, *365 Ways to Say "I Love You" to Your Kids*, *The One-Year Life Verse Devotional*, and the acclaimed modern parable *Once Upon a Tandem*. Jay and his high-school sweetheart, Rita, have four sons, one daughter, and three daughters-in-law and live in St. Charles, Illinois. You can read his weekly dadblog at jaypayleitner.com.

The National Center for Fathering

We believe *every* child needs a dad they can count on. At the National Center for Fathering, we inspire and equip men to be the involved fathers, stepfathers, grandfathers, and father figures their children need.

The National Center was founded by Dr. Ken Canfield in 1990 as a non-profit scientific and education organization. Today, under the leadership of CEO Carey Casey, we continue to provide practical, research-based training and resources that reach more than one million dads annually.

We focus our work in four areas, all of which are described in detail at fathers.com:

Research. The Personal Fathering Profile, developed by a team of researchers led by Ken Canfield, and other ongoing research projects provide fresh insights for fathers and serve as benchmarks for evaluating the effectiveness of our programs and resources.

Training. Through Championship Fathering Experiences, Father-Daughter Summits, online training, small-group curricula, and train-the-trainer programs, we have equipped over 80,000 fathers and more than 1000 trainers to impact their own families and local communities.

Programs. The National Center provides leading edge, turnkey fathering programs, including WATCH D.O.G.S. (Dads Of Great Students), which involves dads in their children's education and is currently in more than 1300 schools in 36 states. Other programs include Fathering Court, which helps dads with significant child-support arrearages, and our annual Father of the Year Essay Contest.

Resources. Our website provides a wealth of resources for dads in nearly every fathering situation, many of them available free of charge. Dads who make a commitment to *Championship Fathering* receive a free weekly e-newsletter full of timely and practical tips on fathering. *Today's Father*, Carey Casey's daily radio program, airs on 600-plus stations. Listen to programs online or download podcasts at fathers.com/radio.

Make your commitment to Championship Fathering

Championship Fathering is an effort to change the culture for today's children and the children of coming generations. We're seeking to reach, teach, and unleash 6.5 million dads, creating a national movement of men who will commit to LOVE their children, COACH their children, MODEL for their children, ENCOURAGE other children, and ENLIST other dads to join the team. To make the Championship Fathering commitment, visit fathers.com/cf.

Also by Jay Payleitner

52 Things Kids Need from a Dad
What Fathers Can Do to Make a Lifelong Difference

Good news—you are already the perfect dad for your kids! Still, you know you can grow. In the pages of this bestseller, Jay Payleitner, veteran radio producer and dad of five, offers a bounty of inspiring and unexpected insights:

- *straightforward rules*: "carry photos of your kids," "Dad tucks in," and "kiss your wife in the kitchen"
- *candid advice that may be tough to hear*: "get right with your own dad," "throw out your porn," and "surrender control of the TV remote"
- *weird topics that at first seem absurd*: "buy Peeps," "spin a bucket over your head," and "rent a dolphin"

Surely, God—our heavenly Father—designed fatherhood to be a joy, a blessing, and a blast! *A great gift or men's group resource.*

365 Ways to Say "I Love You" to Your Kids

Expressions of love can get lost in the crush of carpools, diaper changes, homework, and afterschool activities. But Jay Payleitner is here to help you turn the dizzying array of activities into great memories. Learn to say "I love you"…

> …*at bedtime…in the car…in different languages… without words…doing chores…when your kids mess up big time…on vacation…using secret phrases…in crazy unexpected ways…in everyday life…in ways that point to God.*

Whether your kids are newborn or college-bound, these 365 simple suggestions—from silly to serious—will help you lead your precious pack to joy, laughter, and connection one "I love you" at a time.

52 Things Daughters Need from Their Dads
What Fathers Can Do to Build a Lasting Relationship

The days of tea parties, stuffed doggies, and butterfly kisses are oh-so-important, but they don't last forever. So how can a dad safeguard his daughter so she grows up strong, healthy, beautiful, and confident?

Jay Payleitner has given valuable, man-friendly advice to thousands of dads in his bestselling *52 Things Kids Need from a Dad*. Now Jay guides you into what may be unexplored territory—*girl land*—and gives you ways to...

- date your daughter
- be on the lookout for "hero moments" and make lasting memories
- protect her from eating disorders and other cultural curses
- scare off the scoundrels and welcome the young men who might be worthy
- give your daughter a positive view of men

Jay will help you feel encouraged with 52 creative ideas to give you confidence in relating to your precious daughter...in ways that will help her blossom into the woman God has designed her to be.

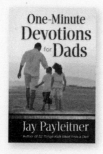

One-Minute Devotions for Dads
Lots of dads feel a twinge of terror at the word *devotion*. Something dull and guilt-producing. Something you're supposed to read at 5 a.m. before you do your 100 push-ups and eat your bowl of oat bran.

Enter Jay Payleitner, exit terror. A veteran dad, Jay knows how regular guys think because he is one. His Bible-based coaching sessions—devotions, if you must—offer you unexpected but relevant thoughts and touches of offbeat humor. And "What About You?" wrap-ups leave you with something straightforward to do or think about.

Young dads, older dads—your day will get a shot in the arm from Jay's seasoned wisdom and God-centered thinking.

52 Things Wives Need from Their Husbands
What Husbands Can Do to Build a Stronger Marriage

Nobody knows your wife like you do. You're the guy who can make her day or break her heart. The choice is yours.

If you feel your husband technique could use a quick refresher course, look no further. Jay Payleitner, husband of Rita, veteran dad of five, and author of the bestselling *52 Things Kids Need from a Dad*, offers a bounty of man-friendly advice, such as

- "Stir her pots"
- "Surprise her with sparkly gifts"
- "Be the handyman"
- "Stay married"
- "Kiss her in the kitchen"
- "Leave your mommy"
- "Put her second"

From breakfast to bedtime. For newlyweds to empty-nesters. Here's a great and godly start to winning your wife's heart all over again!

> *"Biblical, fun, wise, and refreshing…*
> *Get it and you'll thank me for having told you about it."*
>
> **—Steve Brown**
> author, professor, and radio teacher on Key Life

Other Helpful Resources from Harvest House

Is That All He Thinks About?
How to Enjoy Great Sex with Your Husband
Marla Taviano

"All he wants is sex, sex, sex!"

If it seems like you and your husband are operating on different wavelengths, there's a good reason for it. God designed the differences between the two of you to draw you together, points out Marla Taviano. So there's a lot you can do to make sex work *for* your relationship. With that positive in mind, Marla helps you...

- stop the "meet my needs; then I'll meet yours" mindset
- expect your husband to act like a man, not like a woman
- celebrate God's plan for you, as a woman, to be godly *and* sexual
- find forgiveness for a wrong sexual past
- discover fun, creative ideas...and a future filled with the pleasure, joy, and closeness you've always hoped for

> *"Buy this book, read it, and do everything Marla says."*
> —**Gabe Taviano**, Marla's husband

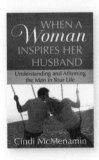

When a Woman Inspires Her Husband
Understanding and Affirming the Man in Your Life
Cindi McMenamin

God created your man with a unique set of qualities and talents. There is no one else in the world like him. And God brought you alongside him in marriage to love and support him as only a wife can. Discover how you can be the encourager, motivator, inspiration, and admiration behind your husband—the wind beneath his wings—as you...

- understand his world
- become his cheerleader

- appreciate his differences
- ease his burdens
- encourage him to dream

Every chapter includes contributions from men who share what they want their wives to know. An uplifting and practical resource designed to strengthen your marriage and create a closer relationship between you and the man you love.

The Husband Project
21 Days of Loving Your Man—on Purpose and with a Plan
Kathi Lipp

- It's about love. It's about respect. It's about letting your husband know you still think he's hot!

- Have you and your husband gone from over-the-top romantics to tolerant roommates?

- Do you dress up more to go out to dinner with your girlfriends than you do to go out with your husband?

- Have you forgotten the fine art of flirting with your guy?

Maybe it's time to put your husband on Project Status.

Kathi Lipp shows you how, even in the midst of your busy schedule, you can take your marriage from *ordinary* to *amazing* in just 21 days. Through simple daily action plans, you'll discover fun and creative ways to bring back that lovin' feeling…and to remind you and your guy why you got married in the first place.